GOD'S

GREAT

EMBRACE

GOD'S GREAT EMBRACE

**Discovering Deeper
Intimacy with *Jesus***

ADRIAN BEST

Ark House Press

Ark House Press
PO Box 1722, Port Orchard, WA 98366 USA
PO Box 1321, Mona Vale, NSW 1660 Australia
PO Box 318 334, West Harbour, Auckland 0661 New Zealand
arkhousepress.com

God's Great Embrace
Written by Adrian Best
Copyright © 2022 by SonRise Life Pty Ltd
godsgreatembrace.com

Unless otherwise indicated, all Scripture quotations are taken from THE HOLY BIBLE, NEW INTERNATIONAL VERSION®, NIV®, copyright © 1973, 1978, 1984, 2011 by Biblica, Inc.® Used by permission. All rights reserved worldwide.

Scripture quotations marked MSG are taken from THE MESSAGE, copyright © 1993, 2002, 2018 by Eugene H. Peterson. Used by permission of NavPress. All rights reserved. Represented by Tyndale House Publishers, Inc.

Scripture quotations marked NASB are taken from the NEW AMERICAN STANDARD BIBLE®, copyright © 1960, 1962, 1963, 1968, 1971, 1972, 1973, 1975, 1977, 1995 by the Lockman Foundation. Used by permission.

Permission to quote or reference other works in *God's Great Embrace* has been granted in writing by the respective publishers. All sources have been properly acknowledged in the bibliographical pages of this publication. Special mention has been requested by: Tyndale House Publishers (Some content taken from Abba's Child by Brennan Manning. Copyright © 1994, 2002, 2015. Used by permission of NavPress. All rights reserved. Represented by Tyndale House Publishers, a Division of Tyndale House Ministries); Kregel Publications (Excerpted from 101 Hymn Stories by Kenneth W. Osbeck © 2012. Used by permission of Kregel Publications); Zondervan (Some content taken from Expository Sermons on Revelation by W.A. Criswell. Copyright © 1963 by Zondervan. Used by permission of Zondervan. Some content taken from PROOF by Daniel Montgomery and Timothy Paul Jones. Copyright © 2014 by Daniel Montgomery and Timothy Paul Jones. Used by permission of Zondervan. Some content taken from Best-Loved Hymn Stories by Robert Harvey. Copyright © 1963 by Zondervan. Used by permission of Zondervan); The CS Lewis Company Ltd (The Weight of Glory by CS Lewis © copyright CS Lewis Pte Ltd 1949).

Cataloging-in-Publication Data
Best, Adrian, 1974-
    God's great embrace : discovering deeper intimacy with Jesus
    / Adrian Best
    Includes bibliographical references.
    Includes index.
    ISBN 978-0-6488873-8-6 (paperback)
    1. Union with Christ. 2. Grace (Theology). 3. Faith. 4. Christian life. 5. Spiritual growth. 6. Trinity. I. Title.

This title is also available as an e-book and audiobook.

ISBN: 978-0-6488873-8-6 (paperback)
ISBN: 978-0-6450153-6-2 (e-book)
ISBN: 978-0-6450153-9-3 (audiobook)

Cover design by Anna Maley-Fadgyas. bookdesigns.com.au
Cover photo courtesy of shutterstock.com [ID 33495982].
Illustrations by Aurélia Chaintreuil. aurelia-art.com Illustrations based on 1. Cover design (opening title page).
2. Photo courtesy of Eloise Allbury (page 48). 3. Photos courtesy of istockphoto.com (pages 33 [ID 185253647],
99 [ID 182668143], 110 [ID 466268089]).
Layout by bookdesigns.com.au and initiateagency.com

In loving memory of
Amelie Sophia Best and
David Reginald Best

Contents

Acknowledgments

I'd like to offer a word of thanks to:

Heidi—my sweetheart, best friend and precious wife: This book would not have been written without your support. Thank you for all your love, patience, encouragement and prayers. You've sacrificed a lot so this book might see the light of day.

Téa, Elijah, and Christelle—my three young children: You delight my heart and your little lives have helped shape this book.

Alison—my mom: Your unconditional love and support means more to me than you'll ever know.

Rev. Dr. John Yates—my dear friend and longtime mentor: Your Jesus-centered, Trinitarian approach to theology and life has left an indelible impression on me. I'm deeply grateful.

James Newman, Nicole Danswan, Lynn Goldsmith and the rest of the team at Ark House Press: Thank you for publishing this book. Your processes and commitment epitomize industry standard excellence.

Thomas Womack and Kathy Ide: Without your editorial expertise this book would not be what it is today. Your professionalism, advice, attention to detail and incisive reworking of text is second to none.

Aurélia Chaintreuil: Your graphite artwork in this book is exquisite.

Anna Maley-Fadgyas: Your cover looks incredible.

My beta readers—Sace Buma, Amy Ridley, Steven Pyle, Penny Mimmie Ng, Richard McAllister, Matthew Easter, Anne-Elise Charles, Deborah Uselioates, Sarah Chapman, Andrew Broadbent, Serena Francis, Laura Otto and Caroline Khoo: You gave generously of your time to read and respond to the draft of this book. I'm filled with gratitude to you all for your helpful comments.

My friends who provided personal stories: May your real-life experience of union with Christ help people to share more deeply in the life of Jesus.

And to you, the reader: I'm honored that you read this book. I've been praying for you since before you even knew about this book. I asked God to prepare your heart so that you might be captivated and transformed by the wonder and mystery of your union with Christ.

May the God and Father of our Lord Jesus Christ be glorified in all our lives.

Adrian Best

Introduction

Life Is All About Jesus

To get a glimpse of how different our lives could be if we grasped the truths explored in this book, imagine hearing a testimony like this nearly two thousand years ago:

> *We've seen things.* Breathtaking, astonishing things. But our hearts have pierced the veil and seen what even our eyes cannot. Revelations from God, declaring that inexhaustibly awesome wonders have taken place in Jesus Christ.
>
> "Moses, the prophets, truly the whole of Scripture points to me," our Lord said to us. "I am the bread of life. Believe in me and you will never go hungry. I am the way. No one comes to the Father except through me."
>
> When Jesus walked with us, we saw a man. Now we see the eternal plan of God. In the person and work of Christ, all humanity and creation have been renewed. In him, through faith, we've been made new creations, lifted up by the Holy Spirit into the lavishly, loving embrace of God our Father.

We've been described as madmen and fanatics. We're not mad, but we are fanatical about Christ. We live and breathe our Lord Jesus. We're completely immersed in him. He is in us and we in him. He is our life, our work, our purpose, our bread and meat. He's our first thought in the morning, our last thought at night. We worship and adore him—the Prince of Glory, the Son of God.

We seek to know him more and more, and his hold on us grows with each passing day. Therefore, we cannot meet someone without sharing Jesus with that person. It is impossible for us to be silent and idle. Because of this, we have been mocked, despised, lashed, and chained—for him. And if it be the Father's will, we are ready to be crucified for his glory.

What we have, no amount of money can buy. We would rather be slandered and ridiculed, even imprisoned and killed, than deny what we've seen and now believe.

Such are the radical sentiments expressed by the New Testament authors. These individuals had seen something monumental in Jesus. They were bursting at the seams to tell the world about it to help everyone see what they'd seen and to believe what they believed.

To these trailblazers of Christianity, life was all about Jesus. Everything they wrote for us is soaked to the core with him. Beautifully and emphatically they articulated their Christ-centered faith, doing so with clarity and consistency.

They never grew tired of telling everyone that Jesus is our all in all. If we have him, we lack nothing.

These pioneers of the faith had eyes only for Jesus, though they saw through him to his Father. They understood that the whole reason Jesus lived, died and rose again was to take us to the Father. Of course we must center on Jesus, they exhorted, for it's only because of him that we can come to the Father at all. But our focus, they concluded, must be on both Father and Son. We're to know and love them, praise and trust them, obey and glorify them—with all our heart, mind and strength, as inspired in us by the Holy Spirit, whom we're to equally worship as God. Their prism was entirely Trinitarian, but everything they saw was through the lens of Jesus.

More specifically, they viewed themselves as one with Jesus, the Father's beloved Son, the crucified and risen Christ. "Jesus is in us and we're in him. We are united with Christ," they taught. To them, life is all about sharing in the life of Jesus. It's about entering ever more deeply into his intimate relationship with his Abba Father in the Spirit. Intensely meaningful, it is life *in Christ*.

What to Expect from This Book

This book seeks to explore the wonder and mystery of the gospel, the key to all Christian life and practice: the believer's union with Christ.

What is this union? Why is it so important? There are few questions greater than these.

A dear friend and mentor once reminded me that we can't take others where we haven't been ourselves. I want to help you grasp something of your union with Christ by taking you on my own journey. Along the way, we'll encounter some of life's most burning questions. These deep mysteries of life and spirituality are not accessible by science, psychology, or philosophy, but are unveiled in the Trinitarian love and grace of the Father, Son and Holy Spirit poured out for us in Jesus Christ.

I offer my thoughts on union with Christ as a fellow pilgrim to whom God has spoken about this glorious biblical truth through the ups and downs of my life, a good dose of seminary education, and my years of church life, Christian experience and prayer. I've experienced firsthand the truths and the treasures, the pitfalls and the mistakes described in the pages ahead. But this book isn't about me. It's about all believers. It's about the Holy Spirit deepening our journey with Jesus into the Father's heart.

What you'll find here is down-to-earth and pastoral, while also rooted in biblical theology. Starting with foundational truths about this union in the first four chapters, the rest of the book gives rise to an abundance of practical applications, with the potential to transform your life.

Key Terms

Before launching into this book, it's helpful to have a basic working definition of three important concepts associated with union with Christ: sonship, justification and sanctification.

In regard to Jesus, sonship points to his unique relationship with the Father. The sonship of believers refers to our sharing in the Son's relationship with the Father. As God's sons and daughters, we can come before him, just as Jesus does and always has.

In this book, I use the word *sonship* as a theological term. It has nothing to do with gender. Females are brought to sonship in Christ just as males are included in the bride of Christ, the church.

Justification refers to our position before God. We're perfectly righteous in God's sight, totally accepted by him on the basis of Christ's life and cross. Justification takes place the instant we come to faith in Jesus and it remains our status throughout life, despite our sin.

Sanctification describes a life set apart from sin and to God. It refers to the continuing process of being transformed into the likeness of Jesus. We're becoming within ourselves what we already are in Christ. Sanctification progresses gradually throughout life, from conversion until death, with plenty of backward steps and slow advances along the way.

We can rest peacefully in our sonship and justification in Christ, but we must keep a holy dissatisfaction about our current state of sanctification—until that blessed day when we stand before God in heavenly glory, completely and perfectly sanctified in Christ.

1

A Grace Awakening

Have you ever had a light-bulb moment that completely changed the course of your life? An event, big or small, that set you on a radically new path? A moment of realization and inspiration, when lights of insight were switched on for the first time and you saw so clearly things previously hidden in the dark?

For the biggest such moment in my life, I have Martin Luther to thank.

I was in my mid-twenties—my bachelor years—and living with a couple of friends from church. Having had my fill of sitcom TV for the evening, I retired to the modest comforts of my bedroom about nine o'clock. Despite feeling tired and ready for some shut-eye, I felt drawn to an article on Martin Luther that had caught my eye earlier that day at seminary. Lying down, I began to read. I had no idea this article would impact me forever.

Of course, the day I gave my life to Christ at age thirteen was utterly life-changing. That was a spiritual awakening. This was a grace awakening.

The Great Exchange

The article was specifically about Luther's teaching on what he called the "wonderful" or "joyous exchange."[1] I'd never heard of this before, nor of the truth that underpins it—something the article dubbed "union with Christ."

As I pored over the words, God's truth leaped off the pages. My jaw dropped with astonishment and elation. For the first time, the eyes of my understanding saw with clarity, at the heart level, the wonder of God's grace in Christ. In the twinkling of an eye, God deepened my grasp of his gospel. *Salvation is an exchange, through union with Christ.*

This beautiful exchange is summed up by Paul in 2 Corinthians 8:9: "You know the grace of our Lord Jesus Christ, that though he was rich, yet for your sake he became poor, so that you through his poverty might become rich."

And again, in 2 Corinthians 5:21: "God made him who had no sin to be sin for us, so that in him we might become the righteousness of God."

The climax of this exchange is found in Ephesians 1:3: "Praise be to the God and Father of our Lord Jesus Christ, who has blessed us in the heavenly realms with every spiritual blessing in Christ."

Here's Paul's point: What is ours is given to Jesus, and what is his is given to us.

Christ became one of us, fulfilled the law and all righteousness, and on the cross took upon himself and dealt with every fallen aspect of our lives—all our sin and guilt, brokenness and shame, judgment and eternal death—in order that we, united with him, may have bestowed on us every good thing of Christ's—his sonship and glory, righteousness and holiness, joy and eternal life, and more.

Luther used the picture of marriage to illustrate this truth.[2] All that the bride is and has, she shares with her groom; all that the groom is and has, he shares with his bride (Song of Songs 2:16). So it is with us and our Bridegroom, to whom we're joined in the most perfect of all marriages.

Now, imagine that the bride is a prostitute and the groom is a king. Full of grace and love, the king says to her, "All that you are and have, I take to myself, and all I am and have, I give to you, my queen."

That is what it means to be in Christ.

Whatever Christ shares with us is truly and uniquely his own. Jesus gives us his sonship, his righteousness, his sanctification. It would be wrong to think of Christ's sonship *and* our sonship, or Christ's righteousness *and* ours, or Christ's holiness of life *and* ours. There aren't two sonships, two justifications, two sanctifications. Christ's sonship is our adoption, his righteousness is our righteousness, his sanctification is our sanctification. His becomes ours.

Likewise, it's wrong to think God treats us "as if" we're his children or "as if" we're righteous. If you're united with Christ, you *are* a child of God and you *are* righteous.

Whatever has happened to Jesus has also, in him, happened to us. His history is our history. It's the exchange of our fallen humanity for his risen and glorified humanity. It's the exchange of our dead existence in sin for his fellowship with the Father in the Spirit. To be a Christian is to share in the life of Jesus.

The Time Between Times

That article enabled me to see the beauty and joy of Christianity in ways I never had before.

As I set it on my bedside table, something further dawned on me. If the great exchange is true, our salvation in Christ is already complete.

When viewed from the perspective of God, who is outside time, Christians are even now united with Christ in all his fullness. God gave us all of Christ's benefits at once, in the moment we first had faith and were made one with his Son (Romans 8:30; 1 Corinthians 6:11; Ephesians 1:3–14; Hebrews 10:14). As Paul says, "In Christ you have been brought to fullness" (Colossians 2:10). In love, the Father has given all things to Jesus (John 3:35), and all things of Jesus are given to those who believe (Ephesians 1:3).

From God's vantage point, all the various aspects of salvation—our adoption, justification, sanctification and glorification—continue simultaneously in our lives from conversion onward. Each is like the facet of a diamond, and the diamond is Christ, whom we received at first faith.

But from our perspective, governed as we are by time, salvation is perceived and experienced in stages as a linear progression or in chronological order: faith followed by adoption and justification, followed by sanctification, then glorification. We're acutely aware of the distinction between what we are already in Christ (adopted, righteous, sanctified and glorified) and what we are in ourselves (sorely in need of sanctification and glorification).

To our time-locked thinking:

- we have been saved (from the punishment and reign of sin and to God's embrace)
- we are being saved (from the power and influence of sin at work within us and to God's likeness)
- we ultimately will be saved (from the lingering presence of sin in us and to God's glory)

We presently experience Christ's resurrection life and power in part, not in full. We're in the time between times—between Christ's first and second comings. But at Christ's glorious return, we will experience his fullness in us. When we see him, we'll be like him (1 John 3:2).

God sees the end from the beginning. He knows the overall plan, the whole canvas, with all its intricacies. He's a weaver of tapestries who creates the tiniest detail and designs the big picture. We, on the other hand, cannot see the end from the beginning. That is why we worry about our salvation and need our Father's constant reassurance to strengthen our faith and hope.

We ask God, "Father, do you love me?"

"Yes," he replies. "More than you can imagine. I chose you before the creation of the world to be my child."

"Do you love me even when I sin?"

"Yes, even then."

"So, I'm forgiven?"

"Yes, of every single sin."

"So then... I'm right in your sight?"

"Yes. Perfectly righteous."

"Will you make me more like Jesus?"

"Yes. I will sanctify you."

"And will you keep me, protect me, and lead me home to heavenly glory?"

"Yes, yes and yes. Those whom I have chosen, I also called; those I called, I also justified; those I justified, I also glorified. All my promises are Yes in Christ, and all are yours in Christ." (Romans 8:30; 2 Corinthians 1:20).

Paradigm Shift

From that evening onward, my Christian walk took a new direction. I was determined to understand more deeply the believer's union with Christ and the great exchange it brings about. I saw this doctrine as crucial gospel truth in which to grow.

2

The Gospel in Two Words

I love to go hiking, away from the hustle and bustle of civilization. I've found no better place to relax, unwind, ponder and pray than out on a nature trail where my five senses can enjoy the freedom of the great outdoors.

On nearly every trail I hike, seeds are scattered all around me. I glimpse them, yet I don't pay attention to them. My brain focuses on the bigger picture and omits these lesser things.

But when I think about them, these little bundles of nature amaze me. In humble seeds lie the power to grow an entire forest.

A Duet of Words

Key details can be right in front of our eyes, yet we fail to see them. That's especially true if the details are small. Little things often go unnoticed. Obscured by bigger things more easily perceived, they seem insignificant. But great truths can be hidden in small details.

Like a humble seed, there's a little phrase in the Bible that often goes unnoticed. We hear it in church and we read it on nearly every page of the New Testament epistles, yet we often view it as unimportant, uninteresting, or as time-worn Christian jargon.

But there's far more to this little phrase than we could ever imagine. In it, infinitely great things are found. It contains a mountain of meaning and tons of power. It's the Bible's abbreviation for the profound truth and reality of the believer's union with Christ.

That phrase is *in Christ*.

God's wisdom is packaged in those two words (1 Corinthians 1:30). God designed salvation in such a way that in order for us to share in Christ's wondrous blessings, Jesus himself must dwell in us and we in him (Romans 8:10; 1 Corinthians 1:30). We must be one with him—united with Christ (Romans 6:5). In this duet of words, Scripture finds its shorthand for all the marvel and mystery of the Christian life.

The phrase *in Christ* (and its variations, *into Christ, with Christ, through Christ*) can be seen a staggering number of times in the New Testament. It undoubtedly held great meaning for the Bible's authors.

The apostle Paul used this expression a whopping 216 times in his writings.[3] In the opening of Ephesians (1:1–14), he uses *in Christ* (or its sister phrases) over ten times in just thirteen verses. That's intense—especially when we consider he uses the common word *and* fewer times in the same passage.

Peppering his letters to the early church with these phrases, Paul tells us that we:

- have grace in Christ (1 Corinthians 1:4;
  Ephesians 1:6; 2 Timothy 1:9)
- have been blessed with every spiritual blessing in
  Christ (Ephesians 1:3)
- have been chosen in Christ (Ephesians 1:4, 11)
- have been created in Christ (Ephesians 2:10)
- are new creations in Christ (2 Corinthians 5:17)
- have died with Christ (Romans 6:3–11;
  Galatians 2:20; Colossians 2:12, 20; 3:3;
  2 Timothy 2:11)
- have risen with Christ (Romans 6:4–11;
  Ephesians 2:6; Colossians 2:12; 3:1)
- have been made alive in Christ (Romans 6:8, 11;
  Colossians 2:13; 2 Timothy 2:11)
- have been seated in the heavenly places in Christ
  (Ephesians 2:6)
- are reigning with Christ (2 Timothy 2:12)
- have redemption in Christ (1 Corinthians 1:30;
  Ephesians 1:7)
- have adoption (sonship) in Christ (Ephesians
  1:5; Galatians 3:26)
- have justification (righteousness) in Christ
  (Galatians 2:17; 1 Corinthians 1:30;
  2 Corinthians 5:21)
- have sanctification (holiness) in Christ
  (1 Corinthians 1:2, 30; Ephesians 2:10)
- have glorification in Christ (Romans 8:17)
- have wisdom in Christ (1 Corinthians 1:30)
- have eternal life in Christ (Romans 6:23)

- have an inheritance in Christ (Ephesians 1:13–14; Romans 8:17)
- have been marked with the seal of the Holy Spirit in Christ (Ephesians 1:13)

Paul is so prolific in his use of the phrase *in Christ* that theologian Albert Schweitzer says, "This 'being-in-Christ' is the prime enigma of the Pauline teaching: once grasped it gives the clue to the whole."[4] From beginning to end, union with Christ is the heart of Paul's Christian life, theology and experience.

Writing of Paul, the esteemed Scottish minister James S. Stewart described union with Christ as "the key which unlocks the secrets of his soul," even more than justification, sanctification, or reconciliation. Stewart continues:

> If one seeks for the most characteristic sentences the apostle ever wrote, they will be found not where he is refuting the legalists, or vindicating his apostleship, or meditating on eschatological hopes, or giving practical ethical guidance to the church, but where his intense intimacy with Christ comes to expression.[5]

And Paul isn't the only one. According to priest and author Brennan Manning, "Union with Jesus emerges as John's dominant theme" in his Gospel account,[6] a point with which eminent theologian Martyn Lloyd-Jones agrees.[7]

The doctrine of union with Christ pervades the whole New Testament. As theologian Sinclair Ferguson says, the believer's union with Christ is "a doctrine which lies at the heart of the Christian life" and "the truth to which the New Testament constantly returns."[8]

Many founding fathers of Protestantism and other historic figures in the church over the last five hundred years have taught union with Christ in their sermons and writings. Pastors, theologians and missionaries—including giants of the faith like Martin Luther, John Calvin, John Owen, Jonathan Edwards, Charles Spurgeon, Hudson Taylor, Karl Barth and John Stott—have taught about our union with Christ.

Christianity 101

Having studied this doctrine at PhD level, I'm convinced that union with Christ is Christianity 101. Along with the cross, it's the central truth of the entire doctrine of salvation.[9]

To be saved is to be in Christ; to be born again is to be in union with Jesus. The phrase *in Christ* is virtually a synonym for "Christian" in 2 Corinthians 12:2 ("I know a man in Christ") and Romans 16:7 ("Andronicus and Junia, my fellow Jews who… were in Christ before I was").[10]

If you believe in Jesus as your Lord and Savior, you are in union with him. You're united with Christ irrespective of how close you feel to him on any given day. The depth of your experience of intimacy with Jesus may fluctuate and your devotion to fellowship with him may vary, but your union with him remains constant and complete.

Nothing can make you any more or any less united with Christ. It's like marriage. You're either married or you're not. No one can become more married or less married. You may sometimes feel closer to your spouse than you do at other times, but the marriage covenant doesn't fluctuate based on emotions.

Union with Christ is the way God works in us and through us. It's not a single blessing among many other parts of our salvation. We receive adoption, justification, sanctification and glorification when we become one with Jesus through faith.

As Paul says in Ephesians 1:3, in Christ we receive "every spiritual blessing." All the benefits of salvation radiate from this union. Like wheel spokes extending from the hub, union with Christ is at the center of it all.

The Great Irony

Although every believer is in union with Christ, some don't know it, or know it only vaguely. They miss out on the incredible added dimension of daily Christian experience that comes from living consciously in union with Christ. They're not dwelling in the security, peace and power of the revelation of what it means to be united with Jesus.

Imagine peering through the lens of a high-power camera. You zoom in on a fairyfly, the world's tiniest insect—some are only 0.005 inches long (0.13 mm). It sits delicately on a shiny golden surface. You see the long bristles on the fairyfly's wings, giving it a kind of feathery appearance.

Now visualize yourself slowly zooming out. The golden surface curves in a circular fashion and you see a person's face imprinted in the gold. You decipher that it's a coin. Widening the scope further, you realize this coin is nestled among countless other gold coins, plus gems and precious jewels. The fairyfly has no idea that a priceless treasure lies beneath its feet.

Christians who are unaware of their union with Christ are sitting on a great treasure without realizing it.

If you're a Christian, you've been in union with Jesus from the moment you first committed your life to him. All the wonder and mystery of this truth has been yours since your conversion.

Fixing the Lens

Until we realize the central place of union with Christ in Christian theology, life and practice, many of the gospel's richest treasures will remain hidden from our sight and experience. "Union with Christ may be the most important doctrine you never knew you needed to know."[11]

3

The Dynamic of God

Before we explore the tremendous wonders of life in Christ, let's first consider its mystery. We'll begin with a glimpse through the eyes of a fisherman named John.

Our boat cut smoothly through tranquil shallows, waves gently lapping the wooden bow. The whisper of wind in the sails and the songs of seabirds in flight were like music to my ears. I took in a long, deep breath, refreshed by the crisp air and the familiar scent of open water. Flanked by my friend Peter and my brother James, I looked fondly at my Lord and my fellow disciples. Then I followed Jesus's gaze and peered into the distance to the lake's far side.

When we pushed off from shore, the sun was slowly retiring. But as we sailed, the sky quickly darkened as billowing black clouds rolled in. A strong wind rose. This had the makings of a raging tempest.

My Lord was resting in the stern, asleep. And rightly so. His ministry was taxing, though he went about it with tremendous grace, peace and strength.

Like a monster let loose from the deep, the fierce storm struck and ravaged us. Lightning filled the sky. Winds growled, rain and waves battered us, more violent than anything we'd ever seen. Twelve grown men shouted with dread, though our voices were drowned out by the howls of nature's fury.

We all battled desperately to keep afloat, but the deck was swamped. Timbers groaned as if at breaking point. This would surely be our end.

I glanced back at the stern. Incredibly, Jesus slept calmly on a cushion.

"Lord!" I yelled at the top of my lungs. "We're going to drown!"

He opened his eyes and rose.

With a single word, Jesus tamed the monster. In the blink of an eye, all was calm. Still. The waters flat.

He turned to us in loving rebuke. "Why are you so afraid? Where is your faith?"

We looked at one another in amazement. *Who is this,* I wondered, *that even the winds and waves obey him?*

We sailed on to the region of the Gerasenes, across the lake from Galilee. Dawn's approach was barely perceptible when we disembarked.

In the dim light, a path led to the border of an old graveyard, misty from the recent storm. All was eerily quiet. The only sound was our shuffling feet on the lakeshore as we awaited direction.

What did our Lord want here, on this side of the lake, at this hour?

A hand squeezed my shoulder. I turned to see Jesus at my side. He smiled, as if he'd heard my thoughts and was offering reassurance.

"Let's go," he said, motioning us toward a hillside.

At a bend in the path, I heard a rustle, then a cackle and a screech. I stared into the misty darkness. Something moved beyond the haze. I froze with fear. Someone lurked among the scattered tombs. I shuddered.

The other disciples stood alert but silent.

A naked man leaped out of the darkness. Deathly thin, he lurched toward us, body writhing. Fingers at the tips of contorted arms curled like claws. He foamed at the mouth, his eyes wild. His wrists and ankles were ringed in scars. His arms and legs bore gashes and welts.

Just yards from us, his onrush halted. He cursed and screamed with devilish rage.

My heart pounded, my knees quivered, my mouth went bone dry. A quick sideward glance confirmed that the others were as scared as I was.

All but one.

Jesus strode straight toward the possessed man. Clearly he'd come here for this very encounter. As he stepped past me, I sensed his compassion.

"Come out of this man, you impure spirit!" Jesus commanded.

The madman fell to his knees. "What do you want with me, Jesus, Son of the Most High God?" he shouted at the top of his voice. "I beg you, don't torture me!"

"What is your name?" Jesus asked.

"My name is Legion, for we are many."

The man pointed to the hillside, where a huge swine herd occupied a high slope. "If you drive us out," he begged Jesus, "send us into the pigs."

"Go!" Jesus commanded.

At once, the whole herd convulsed. Pigs charged down the steep bank and plunged into the lake, where they could only drown.

When the violent thrashing of waters ceased, I returned my gaze to the man possessed.

He sat now before Jesus, a picture of peace, in full control of mind and body.

During our return journey across the lake, I reflected on these extraordinary events. How on earth did Jesus cast out a legion of demons and restore that afflicted soul?

And how on earth did he calm a raging tempest?

Jesus had not been afraid of the madman or of the storm, both of which had filled the twelve of us with fear.

As months passed, I spent more time with Jesus, watching him and listening intently. Following his death and resurrection, the Holy Spirit whom Jesus sent testified to us about him. And the answers to my questions became clear.

I'd thought God sent his Son to earth to go it alone. But no. They had remained in constant relationship the entire time. I'd been watching the unique union of Father, Son and Holy Spirit.

No Solo Act

Throughout Jesus's life, people wondered who he was. Some thought Jesus was John the Baptist, others Elijah, Jeremiah, or one of the prophets (Matthew 16:13–14; Mark 8:27–28; Luke 9:18–19). Others, like Nicodemus, viewed Jesus as God's appointed teacher (John 3:1–2). Many thought they were watching a prophet or a wonder-worker. Peter, having divine insight, believed Jesus to be the Christ, the incarnate Son of God (Matthew 16:15–16; Mark 8:29–30; Luke 9:20).

Today, numerous Christians believe that Jesus of Nazareth was able to perform miracles because he is God. His power to work signs and wonders as he walked this earth is viewed as the power of his divine nature as the second person of the Trinity.

But many Christian theologians believe, on the basis of passages like Philippians 2:6–7, that Jesus "emptied himself" of his exercise of divine power. Though he remained fully God and retained all of his divine ability, power and glory as the second person of the Trinity, Jesus chose not to exercise any of it for human living. Jesus did this so that he might thoroughly identify with us in our humanity. Though he was and is the second person of the Trinity, Jesus was and is as human as you and I (John 1:14; Hebrews 2:14–18; 4:15; Philippians 2:7; Romans 8:3). Consequently, Jesus of Nazareth was dependent on the Father and he relied on the Holy Spirit.

In fact, what the disciples and others were watching was the Trinity in action. The incarnate Son lived life and fulfilled his ministry from a place of union with his Father and the Holy Spirit. "I and the Father are one," Jesus said (John 10:30; 17:11, 22)—one in both being and action.

Jesus himself testified:

> Anyone who has seen me has seen the Father. How can you say, "Show us the Father"? Don't you believe that I am in the Father and that the Father is in me? The words I say to you I do not speak on my own authority. Rather, it is the Father, living in me, who is doing his work. Believe me when I say that I am in the Father and the Father is in me. (John 14:9–11; see also John 12:49–50; 14:20; 17:21, 23)

> The Son can do nothing by himself; he can do only what he sees his Father doing, because whatever the Father does, the Son also does. For the Father loves the Son and shows him all he does. (John 5:19–20; see also John 8:28–29)

Such is the profound oneness and intimacy of Son and Father. Jesus trusted the Father to show him his will and to enable him to live and to work in the power of the Holy Spirit.

Jesus was as one with the Holy Spirit as he was with the Father. He was conceived by the Spirit (Matthew 1:18, 20; Luke 1:35). Throughout Jesus's formative years, the Spirit enabled him to grow in wisdom and strength and in favor with God and people (Luke 2:40, 52). The Father "anointed" Jesus with the Spirit (Acts 10:38); the Spirit was "on Jesus" (Matthew 3:16; Mark 1:10; Luke 3:22; John

1:32) and "remained on him" (Luke 4:18; John 1:32–33; Isaiah 61:1–2).

The Spirit was not simply *on* Jesus but *in* him. Jesus was "full of the Holy Spirit" (Luke 4:1). He had the Spirit "without limit" (John 3:34). Consequently, he was "led by the Spirit" (Matthew 4:1; Mark 1:12). He resisted the devil by the Holy Spirit's power (Luke 4:1–14). He went about his daily life and ministry "in the power of the Spirit" (Luke 4:14). The words he spoke, the good news he proclaimed, the good he did, the miracles he performed, the captives he set free—even his fullness of joy—all these things and more, Scripture tells us, Jesus accomplished by the Spirit (Matthew 12:18, 28; Luke 4:17–21; 10:21; John 6:63; Acts 1:1–2; 10:38).

It was by the Spirit that Jesus offered himself up to die on a cross (Hebrews 9:14). And by this same Spirit, the Father raised him from the dead (Romans 8:11; 1 Peter 3:18).

The Holy Spirit was Jesus's inseparable companion throughout his entire human life, from conception to glorification. Anyone who saw or heard Jesus was watching the Trinity that eternally was and is and forever will be.

We see this Trinitarian dynamic throughout Scripture. The Father is the origin and source of God's plan and action. From the Father are all things, and to him are all things. The Son is the content and reality of God's plan and action. The Holy Spirit brings God's plan and action into existence. Whether in creation, redemption, or every activity of God in our lives, all things proceed from the Father, are given in and through the Son, and are enabled by the Spirit. And all things return to and for the Father, in and through the Son, by the Spirit.

The Father, Son and Holy Spirit act as one because they *are* one. There is only one God, and God is a Trinity—three persons in a single essence or being. Each one is in the other two. They exist together in an eternal fellowship of mutual love, living the one life, moving and working as one. None of the persons of the Godhead exists separately from the others. Every work of God is a unified action of all three persons. What the Father does, the Son does, as does the Spirit.

Unfortunately, many Christians separate the persons of the Trinity in their minds. They compartmentalize God's activity in time, narrowly viewing the Father as creator, the Son as redeemer, and the Holy Spirit as transformer. There's truth in that. The Father did create the heavens and the earth. The Son did take on human flesh, live among us for thirty-three years and die on a cross to save us. The Spirit does indwell and empower us for Christian living. But God's work in history is not a series of solo acts, as if the Father worked, then the Son worked, and now the Spirit works.

The disciples saw Jesus calm the storm and cast out Legion, but those miracles were equally a work of the Father and of the Spirit. Jesus did those things as a human dependent on the Father, trusting his Father to work in and through him, in the power of the Holy Spirit.

That's why Jesus didn't fear the storm or the demon-possessed man, nor did he ever doubt the outcome in those situations. He had already seen his Father cross the lake and heal that oppressed man. His Father had told him, "Go to the other side of the lake and release the tormented soul." To which Jesus responded, "If my Father has said it, it will be! Nothing can stop it from coming to pass. No wave is too big, no wind too strong, no rain too heavy, no demon too evil. If my Father has said that I'll get to the other side of the lake and free the captive—then so it will be!"

Such was his trust and expectation in the Father as his source of authority (John 5:19; 12:49; 14:10).

This mind-bending mystery of the union that exists between the Father, Son and Holy Spirit is far beyond the realm of any human intellect, logic, or reason. All we can do is sit back in awe and celebrate our triune God.

Union Versus Diversity in Relationships

Our finite minds can fathom only relationships based on two separate things (person with person, person with object, or object with object). These are easy to understand because the two entities have a separate existence and, if living, lead separate lives. For instance, you and a friend, a child and his toy, a bird in a tree, or ink in a pen. This is the matrix of creation. When God, in his infinite wisdom, created the universe, he saw fit to put all things in relation to one another—from its tiniest building blocks to its galactic giants and everything in between. Every relation you see or experience in life falls into this category of diversity.

All, that is, except one. A Christian's relationship with God is not a diversity but a union.

A union is far more difficult to understand than a diversity because the persons involved are one, yet distinct, and they live the one life. Thankfully, the Bible provides insight. Our union with Christ follows the same Trinitarian dynamic as seen in God: from the Father, through the Son, by the Spirit, for the Father.

4

One with Jesus

S ome things in life will drive us as mad as a hatter if
we try to comprehend them fully. We might be able
to say a certain amount about a perplexing thing, but
unanswerable questions and unfathomable aspects remain.
Look at the image below.

What do we know about this image? Well, it's a triangular arrangement of cubes. But if we attempt to work out its spatial orientation, we can drive ourselves crazy.

The same can be said about our union with Christ. There's a certain amount we know—whatever God has revealed in Scripture. But there's plenty that remains an enigma, a mystery. If we try to explain details that God in his wisdom has chosen to keep hidden, we'll go nuts.

Yet the doctrine of our union with Christ is the key to all Christian life and practice. It is "as fundamental to the Christian life as it is stretching to the Christian's mind."[12] So we're wise to at least try to grasp its truth, even though our understanding of it will be modest at best.

With this in mind, I want to venture into the study of our union with Christ as simply as possible. We'll begin with Paul's analogy of marriage, then look at Jesus's analogy of the vine and the branches, then humbly delve deeper into Scripture.

A Marriage Made in Heaven

The relationship between husband and wife is intensely intimate. Paul says, "A man will leave his father and mother and be united to his wife, and the two will become one flesh" (Ephesians 5:31). Paul is quoting God's words found in Genesis 2:24 (as Jesus did in Matthew 19:5 and Mark 10:7–8). Husband and wife are so intertwined that, in a sense, they become one.

After quoting those words from Genesis, Paul makes his point clear: "This is a profound mystery—but I am talking about Christ and the church" (Ephesians 5:32). Paul compares marriage to the relationship between Christ and the church. Marriage is the most intimate interpersonal relationship known to humanity. It's a concept we can easily identify with and readily comprehend. Paul uses it as an analogy to convey a picture of the supreme intimacy that exists between Christ and believers. We are one, bound together in deep reciprocal love.

Of course, marriage is a faint reflection of the union that exists between Christ and Christians, but it's the closest relationship that creation has to offer as a metaphor for the believer's union with Christ.

The Vine and Its Branches

In John 14:20, Jesus makes a stunning revelation: "I am in my Father, and you are in me, and I am in you." He repeats this mystery and throws light on it by likening his union with believers to that between a vine and its branches. "Abide in me, and I in you... I am the vine, you are the branches; he who abides in me and I in him, he bears much fruit, for apart from me you can do nothing" (15:4–5 NASB).

Here's my paraphrase of what Jesus is saying:

> You dwell in me. You live your life from within me. I am the sphere of your existence. Equally, I dwell in you, living my life in and through you.

The life you live is not your own. You live my life.

I am the true vine and you are my branches. You're one with me. I'm the source of your life. I nourish you, sustain you and maintain you. Just as the branch shares in the life of the vine, so you share in my life.

I am the source of your fruit. The grapes you produce aren't your own; they come from me. You bear my fruit, for you cannot produce fruit apart from me. You are a branch of the living vine, existing in me and producing my fruit as I live in you and through you.

Jesus speaks of us dwelling in him and him in us as our state of being. He uses language of profound intimacy and deep fellowship.

This union is not mysticism (our being absorbed into God). It's interpersonal. Your person is not swallowed up by his. You remain your own person, as does he.

Moreover, we are not one with Christ in the same way that the triune God is one. Christ and the Christian are two distinct beings united as one.

Two Sides of One Coin

Union with Christ involves two fundamental aspects: us in Christ, and Christ in us.

We are in Christ. We're brought into Christ's sphere of existence. We take up residence in him. Our entire being is wrapped up wholly in his. We've been chosen, adopted, justified, sanctified, redeemed and glorified in Christ. Whenever the Father looks upon us, he sees us as one with Jesus, his Son.

Christ is in us. The person of Jesus has taken up residence within us (Romans 8:10; 2 Corinthians 13:5; Colossians 1:27). He works in us from the inside and we live our lives in the reality and realm of his life (Romans 9:1; 15:17–18; 1 Corinthians 9:1; 15:58; 16:24; 2 Corinthians 2:17; 12:19; Ephesians 6:1; Philippians 4:13; Colossians 2:6–7). His life becomes ours.

As Paul declares, "It is no longer I who live, but Christ who lives in me" (Galatians 2:20). "To me, to live is Christ" (Philippians 1:21).

Martin Luther expressed it like this:

> If anyone knocks at the door of my heart and asks, "Who lives here?" I will reply, "Not Martin Luther, but Jesus the Lord."[13]

When someone looks at you, they see both you and Jesus. They might see lots of you and only a little of him, but hopefully, in time, they'll come to see more of him and less of you.

For Christians, being united with Christ is our present and our eternal reality. Our goals now are to celebrate that and to live it. "The mystery in a nutshell," says Paul, "is just this: Christ is in you" (Colossians 1:27 MSG).

Union with Christ's Humanity

Union with Christ can be misunderstood in many ways. Some Christians view it simply as allegiance to Christ or associating with his benefits. Others see it as an intellectual or moral like-mindedness toward Jesus, his teachings and his ethics. To others it's a union of Christ's will and ours, or an imitation of his example, or something we attain only after reaching an exceptional level of personal holiness. Still others think of it as a merging of our essence with Christ's. Then there are those for whom it is merely metaphorical.

Union with Christ is none of those things. It is a life-giving union with the resurrected and glorified Christ. But we must be careful how to interpret this.

Some Christians believe that when Jesus ascended into heaven and was glorified at the Father's right hand, he shed his humanity, leaving only his divine nature. Consequently, they say, Christ comes to us in his divine nature and unites us to his divinity.

But if the humanity of Jesus could be stripped from him at his ascension into heavenly glory, we're doomed. If Jesus is no longer human, we remain lost in our sins because he is no longer one of us.

It's only because Jesus was, is and eternally remains fully human that we can now and forever share in his human life, death, resurrection and glorification for our salvation. The ascended and glorified Christ remains forever fully God and fully human. Whatever else our union with Christ is, it must be a union with his humanity.

Christ Himself Is the Gift

Jesus doesn't give us his riches without giving us himself. He *is* the gift.

Jesus didn't just *obtain* salvation for us, as if he were merely an instrument God used to accomplish our salvation. He *became* salvation for us (1 Corinthians 1:30; Hebrews 5:9).

Salvation isn't merely a transaction in which God declares the believer to be in right relationship with himself on the basis of Christ's work. Rather, salvation is union with the person of Jesus Christ, in whom all the riches of salvation are stored. We receive Jesus with his benefits; we do not receive the benefits alone.

The focus is on Christ himself, not his benefits.

Father and Spirit, Faith and Grace

How is it possible to be united with Christ? How can Jesus in heaven indwell us here on earth?

The Holy Spirit unites us with Christ.

Although God the Father willed and purposed that we be made one with Christ (1 Corinthians 1:30; Ephesians 1:3–14; 2 Timothy 1:9), it's the Spirit that establishes this union (Romans 8:9–11; 1 Corinthians 12:13; Ephesians 3:16–17). The Father gave the Spirit to bring Christ to us.

The same Holy Spirit who was inseparably present in Jesus to anoint, equip, lead and empower him in his redemptive life and work indwells us. He unites us so thoroughly with

Jesus that we may draw from his wellspring every moment of our lives. In this way, the Spirit bestows on us and cultivates in us every benefit of Christ.

Faith unites the believer with Jesus Christ (Ephesians 3:17) in simple childlike trust, like Jesus described in Matthew 18:3. From the moment we first believe in Jesus as Lord and Savior, we're instantly indwelt by the Spirit, who unites us with Christ (Romans 8:9–11).

Union with Christ is God's gift to us. A gift cannot be earned. "It is by grace you have been saved, through faith— and this is not from yourselves, it is the gift of God—not by works, so that no one can boast" (Ephesians 2:8–9). "It is because of [God] that you are in Christ Jesus" (1 Corinthians 1:30; see also Ephesians 1:3–14).

See Jesus First

Union with Christ keeps our focus on Jesus. When you grasp this union at the heart level, you'll see your whole life in him. You'll think of Jesus before you think of yourself. You'll recognize him as the center and circumference of everything. You will view all your needs through his abundance.

When we have that perspective, we'll experience greater freedom, meaning and joy in our day-to-day life. In this book, I want to help you see this for yourself by showing you how Christ meets the deepest needs of the human heart, as he has mine.

Let's begin with identity.

Who Am I?

Personal identity is one of the most universal issues in human existence. We all need to know who we are. Identity provides us with a concept of self and, consequently, a feeling of belonging and acceptance. This is where we gain a sense of security, worth and self-esteem, all requirements for our well-being.

Sadly, many people define themselves by the passions and obsessions of their hearts. They create their identity in terms of their interests, abilities, attributes, assets, accomplishments, successes, or roles in life. Others find identity in their family or friendships, in their ethnicity or nationality, or even in their online profile.

I used to define myself by such things, until I started to see Jesus first. In learning who he is, I learned who I am in him.

5

Our Father Wound

On a recent Father's Day, my two-year-old son, Elijah, scribbled a piece of artwork for me that boasted such incredible color and complexity even the great abstract expressionists of twentieth-century art would've marvelled in admiration.

Not to be outdone by her younger brother, my six-year-old daughter, Téa, handcrafted for me a card trumpeting me as "the bestest daddy in the whole wide world." These words were accompanied by a gorgeous and exquisitely detailed drawing of our family as cartoon pigs. Her artwork could rival the best from Hallmark.

Elijah and Téa—along with my nine-month-old, Christelle—showered me with homemade gifts and a flurry of kisses and cuddles. Then came the great unveiling: a coffee mug decorated with a dozen imprinted photos of Daddy and his children.

One of my greatest hopes as a father is that as my children grow into adulthood, they remember me as a loving daddy who was always there for them, made them feel valued, and wanted only the best for them. I want to fill their hearts with love, to validate them, to make them feel secure and to do them no harm. My reasons are not only paternal, but also spiritual.

Fatherless

Good earthly fathers (biological, step, adoptive, or foster) provide their children with loads of precious memories. If you and your father had a close relationship, you're truly blessed.

But many fathers leave bleeding wounds of the heart.

Perhaps the man who raised you was absent, physically or emotionally. Maybe you didn't really know him because he died or left home before you were old enough to remember. Or you knew him for a limited time. Did your father neglect you? Let you down? Fail you? Lie to you? Break promises? Was he always at work or down at the pub, making you feel as though his career, mates, or booze meant more to him than you?

Did your parents get divorced, leaving your heart aching over a father you didn't see nearly enough? Or when he was home, he didn't pay much attention to you. He was more interested in his TV remote, his personal pursuits, or his busy life than in throwing a ball with you, watching you dance, or listening to your stories.

Maybe your father wasn't affectionate. He had no words of endearment to give you that warm feeling inside that every child craves from their daddy. He might be a genuinely nice guy, but he wasn't the tender fatherly figure you needed. Maybe he never told you he loved you.

Was your father critical or controlling? Demanding, demeaning, or dominating, impossible to please? His words were harsh, his discipline strict. Nothing you did was ever good enough. He compared you with others and you always came up short. Not once did he look you in the eye and say, "I'm proud of you."

Perhaps you and your father had clashing personalities or ideologies. You couldn't see eye to eye with him about anything. Arguments and shouting matches are your most lasting memory of him.

Worst of all is the abusive father. Maybe he erupted like a volcano, with vulgar yelling and flying fists. He may have beaten or raped you, your mother, or your siblings. Or perhaps he subtly manipulated you with demeaning words. Told you he hated you or never wanted you. Whether verbal, physical, emotional, or sexual, the abuse made you feel violated, deeply wounded and dreadfully scarred.

My heart goes out to you. Our earthly fathers are supposed to reflect the character of our heavenly Father, albeit imperfectly.

When fathers cause deep-rooted, lifelong afflictions in the hearts of their children, we call them "father wounds." They can leave a person broken and damaged. Addressing them usually requires considerable prayer, together with pastoral care or professional counseling. Sometimes, therapy with a psychologist or psychiatrist might be the answer.

But the spiritually destructive nature of the father wound is commonly overlooked. A deep father wound can pose a huge obstacle to seeing God as our ever-present, intimate, loving Father.

Father to the Fatherless

If you're struggling to see God as your Father because of how you view your earthly father, your feelings may be so negative and painful that you throw out the whole idea of God's fatherhood. Or perhaps, though you're scarred with hurt and heartache, you try to see God as the Bible depicts him, but you project your earthly father onto God so much that your dominant impression of God encompasses the negative features of your earthly father.

If you're walking down one of these paths, you're not experiencing the beauty and intimacy of knowing God as Father—the Father who enjoys love and life, peace and passion, creativity and glory with his Son. You're missing out on the abounding joy that comes through sharing in their shared life.

God is the only perfect Father (Matthew 5:48; 23:9). He's not *like* a father; he *is* your Father. He's not *a* father, but *the* Father. The "Father to the fatherless" (Psalm 68:5), who heals aching hearts. The Father who loves you with the same measureless love he has for his Son, Jesus.

When we know God as our Father, we know who we truly are.

6

Amelie and the Beloved

Upon delivery at full term, my precious newborn was placed skin-to-skin against my wife's warm chest.

"Amelie, you're beautiful," Heidi cried, her eyes shining with tears, her voice tremulous. "I don't want to lose you!"

Late in the second trimester of pregnancy, doctors diagnosed our child with a severe heart condition. All the brilliance of modern medicine could offer no cure. She would likely die within the first few weeks of life.

The turmoil in my wife's voice cut to the depths of my soul. In incongruous unison, my heart pirouetted with jubilation and collapsed in abject pain. Love mixed with lament.

My little baby girl, wide-eyed in bewilderment of the new world she'd just hurtled into, looked up at me from the warmth and security of Heidi's embrace. The meeting of our eyes cut through all my heartache. Joy eclipsed grief and love eclipsed pain. She was adorable. Seven pounds four ounces of utter cuteness.

Her fragile frame, her soft cheeks and the sweetness of her cooing voice melted my heart. Tears streamed down my cheeks and into my beaming smile.

I wrapped her tiny hand in my big one. "I love you, darling," I whispered.

My daughter was perfect in every way—except for her damaged heart.

The next day, as we prepared to leave King Edward Hospital with our bright-eyed Amelie, Heidi and I asked the pediatrician, "What do we do now?"

"Make family memories. Don't sit at home all day waiting for Amelie to turn. Go out and have fun together. Enjoy her—and let her enjoy you."

And so we did—for five incredible, cherished days.

Amelie experienced our love. She snuggled into us. She felt our caring touch and our butterfly kisses. She smelled our unique scents. She saw our beaming faces. She heard our soft voices and soothing lullabies. She tasted her mommy's milk. These were precious days. But they were not to last.

At noon on her sixth day, Amelie suddenly took a turn for the worse. By nightfall, she entered a time of great suffering. Palliative medical care served to ease her awareness of pain. But nothing could be done about Heidi's and mine.

My Deep Love for Amelie

I had the privilege of spending an hour alone with Amelie. It was the most soul-stirring ordeal I've ever experienced, or likely ever will. Those sixty priceless minutes have shaped not only my fatherhood, but my understanding of the Father-heart of God.

As I cradled my dying daughter tenderly in my arms, her frail lungs clawing for breath, something welled up within my innermost depths that I can only describe as fierce paternal love. My whole being was overwhelmed with a love that was powerful, unfiltered, uninhibited. Stripped of all veneers, preconceptions and distractions.

I've never felt love so pure, despite my countless flaws and imperfections. In that moment I cared for nothing but to cherish my dying darling. I would have done absolutely anything to save this little child from her suffering. My will to protect her was intense.

I looked upon my limp, ashen child. Her once sparkling eyes were now washed out with exhaustion. Yesterday's chubby cheeks were sunken and gaunt. Fighting for life, she occasionally mustered strength enough to grimace or wail in agitation, only to flop back against me like a rag doll moments later.

My crushed heart cried out in a torrent of tears. I felt helpless, paralyzed with inadequacy. I released pent-up prayers of anguish and desperation and hurled them toward the heavens. I took my pain into the very heart of God.

"God, why does Amelie have to die? She's just a baby. If only I could take her place!"

And then, "How much longer must she suffer? Take her now, Lord, for her sake."

By God's grace, a few hours later, Amelie reached her final stage of life. Without agitation or struggle, she lay wrapped in a dainty pink-and-white shawl, taking her last crescendo-decrescendo breaths. She was at peace in Heidi's loving embrace, my arms surrounding both of them. Cuddling her gently, we cried our goodbyes, telling her how much she meant to us and how much we loved her. We prayed for her, committing her spirit to God and thanking him for her life and the blessing she'd been to us.

Finally, we released our daughter to God. "Go, Amelie. Be with Jesus."

Shortly thereafter, God took our daughter home to be with him.

Amelie is and always will be my little girl. She's special to me beyond measure. I loved her before she was born, I cherished her while she was alive and I will treasure her forever. She never had to earn my love. Nothing she did or didn't do could make me love her any more or any less. I don't love her because she was good or innocent, but because she is my child.

That is how our Father loves us—and he loves us even more deeply, though it's impossible for me to imagine.

The Father's Infinite Love for His Son

In Matthew 7:11, Jesus told his followers, "If you, though you are evil, know how to give good gifts to your children, how much more will your Father in heaven give good gifts to those who ask him!"

If I—a human father, broken and blemished in so many ways—am able to love my children with the magnitude I felt for Amelie, how much greater does God the Father love his only begotten Son. I know what it is to love my dying child. Even more does the Father understand how it feels to love his Son, whom he himself sent to die for those who would hate him.

I love my children so deeply that if anyone or anything should ever try to separate them from me, it would be like trying to pry them from the jaws of a ravenous lion. But my fatherly love pales into oblivion compared to the infinite love the Father has for Jesus. And for those of us who are in Christ.

After John baptized Jesus in the River Jordan, as Jesus came up out of the waters, the Father's voice was audibly heard, saying, "This is my Son, whom I love; with him I am well pleased" (Matthew 3:17). Essentially, God was saying:

> Jesus, you are my Son. You're the essence of my essence, the being of my being, even now as you are flesh and blood.
>
> I loved you before the creation of the world and I will love you forever. My love for you is complete, unconditional and selfless. It's perfect, eternal, infinite. It is ultimate love. Pure love. For *I am* love.
>
> Son of my love, I'm pleased with you. Your faithfulness delights me. You're the joy of my heart, the center of my affection, the darling of heaven. You are precious to me beyond description.

We could daisy-chain every worthy superlative and still not come close to capturing the magnitude of the Father's love for Jesus.

And why does the Father love Jesus? One reason alone—because Jesus is his child.

Jesus knew, even as a youngster, that he was God's beloved Son. He declared:

- "My Father loves me" (John 10:17)
- "The Father loves the Son and has placed everything in his hands" (John 3:35)
- "The Father loves the Son and shows him all he does" (John 5:20)

Jesus knew he was the Father's "one and only Son" (John 1:14), "in closest relationship with the Father" (John 1:18), the "beloved" (Matthew 3:17; 17:5), "loved before the creation of the world" (John 17:24).

Jesus knew himself to be the Christ—the Messiah, the Savior of the world. But at his most ontological level, he believed himself to be God's Son. And ultimately that is how he revealed himself to us (see Matthew 11:25–27; Mark 12:1–12; 14:61–62; Luke 2:49; John 5:18; 10:31–39; 12:49–50; 14:1–31; 15:1–27; 16:1–33; 17:1–26; 20:17).

We who are in Christ have the same love from Jesus's Father, and we share in his identity. Brennan Manning said, "In learning who he is, you will find out who you are: Abba's child in Christ our Lord."[14]

7

Abba's Child

Before believing in Jesus, you were a spiritual orphan. But the moment you first accepted Christ as your personal Savior, you were united with him in his sonship. God the Father joined you to his beloved Son, making you his cherished child and himself your loving Father forever (John 1:12–13; Galatians 3:26). "I will be a Father to you," declares the Lord God Almighty, "and you will be my sons and daughters" (2 Corinthians 6:18).

You can't earn this sonship. Adoption in Christ is a free gift from God (Ephesians 1:4–6).

Identity in the Son

What Jesus is by nature, we now are by grace. We're children of God because we're one with Jesus, sharing in his sonship. We share in the Son's relationship with his Father in the power of the Holy Spirit. His Father has become our Father (Matthew 6:9; John 20:17).

That is our true identity. As John declares:

What marvelous love the Father has extended to us! Just look at it—we're called children of God! That's who we really are. (1 John 3:1 MSG)

United with the Son, we have God as our Father in the same way that Jesus does. This is an astounding revelation—perhaps even the climax of the Bible.[15] It's comforting to know and experience God the way Jesus did—as our Abba.

Knowing God as Abba

One of the most penetrating insights into the intimacy between the Father and Son is seen in the Gethsemane prayers of Jesus in the shadow of the cross.

In a cry of impassioned desperation that stretched his filial affection and dependence to the utmost, Jesus called out to his Father.

> They went to a place called Gethsemane, and Jesus said to his disciples, "Sit here while I pray." He took Peter, James and John along with him, and he began to be deeply distressed and troubled. "My soul is overwhelmed with sorrow to the point of death," he said to them. "Stay here and keep watch." Going a little farther, he fell to the ground and prayed that if possible the hour might pass from him. "Abba, Father," he said, "everything is possible for you. Take this cup from me. Yet not what I will, but what you will." (Mark 14:32–36)

The Son, speaking in private with his Father from the depths of his soul, calls him Abba. Until Jesus, God had never been known in such an intimate way.

In Jesus's day, *Abba* was an Aramaic word similar to our English word "Papa," or to a heartfelt "dearest Father." It was a colloquial term used by Jewish children (including adults) when addressing their beloved fathers. It carried a tone of intimacy, warmth and affection. When fully grown children used the term *Abba*, it also conveyed deep reverence and confidence. Both child and father understood that this term of endearment held connotations of the child's dependency and expectancy in Abba to meet his or her every need. It was saturated with a sense of childlike love and trust and with fatherly love and faithfulness.

If the Father is Abba to Jesus, he is no less Abba to those of us who are united with Jesus. We can relate to God as Abba the way Jesus does. And Abba loves us with the same love with which he loves Jesus (John 17:23, 26). Not just to the same *degree* of love—he loves us *in him*. Abba's endless tide of love begins with his Son and flows from him to cascade over us.

Jesus never had to earn Abba's love. Nor do we. Nothing we've done or haven't done, are doing or not doing, or might or might not do, can ever make Abba love us any more or any less. We're immersed in the Father's love for his Son.

The Father's great plan for humanity is to share with us his relationship with Jesus, his beloved Son, so we can by grace enjoy their fellowship forever (Hebrews 2:10–11). That's what salvation is all about. It isn't primarily about forgiveness of sins and getting a ticket to heaven. It's about the Son leaving his Father's glory to come to earth to live, die and rise for us. And to unite himself with us by the Spirit so as to take us back with him to his Father. He did this so that we might enjoy the Father's boundless love as Jesus has always enjoyed it, and so that we can call the Father what Jesus has always called him—Abba—and thus experience the Son's joy for ourselves.

The love Abba has for his children never lets go (Romans 8:38–39). When the eyes of our hearts see this, the gospel becomes truly thrilling.

The Spirit of Sonship

Being able to freely call God "Abba Father" is our greatest privilege in life. But from where does our awareness come that we're Abba's beloved sons and daughters in Christ? It comes from the Holy Spirit, who indwells us and unites us with Christ in his sonship. The Spirit bears witness to our sonship and to Abba's love and inspires us to relate to God as a child relates to her papa—or more accurately, as Jesus relates to his Father.

"The Spirit you received brought about your adoption to sonship," writes Paul. "And by him we cry, 'Abba, Father.' The Spirit himself testifies with our spirit that we are God's children" (Romans 8:15–16). Paul also tells us, "Because you are his sons [and daughters], God sent the Spirit of his Son into our hearts, the Spirit who calls out, 'Abba, Father'" (Galatians 4:6).

The Holy Spirit pours into our hearts the love Abba has for us in his Son (Romans 5:5). The same Spirit who revealed to Jesus the truth about his unique sonship to the Father now brings Christ to us and unites us to him in such a way that we not only are made children of God in him, we also share in the Son's heartfelt knowledge of his sonship and of Abba's great love for him, knowing that what is true of him is true of us in him.

Living as Abba's Child

Jesus found his identity—and his deep sense of love, belonging, approval and self-worth—in one place alone: his sonship to his Abba Father. He didn't look to others for these things. He didn't deliberately seek to be liked by people. He never compared himself with others. He received from the Father every comfort for the soul and all the glory he would ever need (Luke 3:22; John 5:41, 44; 2 Peter 1:17).

We all long to be accepted and valued, but too often we search for these things in the wrong places. We look to other people, hoping that our attributes, careers, accolades, wealth, family and backgrounds will win them over. We depend on others for our inner security, which is an unhealthy and risky way to live.

A mature Christian friend of mine began feeling a deep level of rejection by his peers, which caused him to be tempted to revert to a childhood response of bashing his head against a wall. Instead of focusing on the unwarranted blame and shame, he went to the river and prayed. As he did, God comforted him and gave him a clear sense of blamelessness.

As he relayed his story to me, he asked, "Whose blamelessness was I feeling?"

"Jesus's!" I explained. "The blamelessness of the resurrected Son of God" (see Hebrews 7:26).

No matter how much rejection you experience from people, God will never reject you. He'll restore you in Christ his Son (Ephesians 1:4; Philippians 1:10; Colossians 1:22; 1 Thessalonians 3:13; 5:23; Jude 1:24).

In Christ, we have a Father who loves us unconditionally and accepts us completely, despite our faults and failures. We are the Father's pleasure, pride and joy. We are in Abba's home now and we belong there, just as much as Jesus does.

Perhaps you're not sure these words are true of you. They are. There's no such thing as a second-class Christian. Our Father has no favorites. In Christ there's no distinction, supremacy, or discrimination. All are equal before God. Paul tells us, "In Christ Jesus you are all children of God… There is neither Jew nor Gentile, neither slave nor free, nor is there male and female, for you are all one in Christ Jesus" (Galatians 3:26, 28).

When you fully grasp the truth of your adoption in Christ, you won't care what other people think of you. You won't let their opinions dictate how you feel about yourself. You won't need to prove yourself to anyone (including yourself). You don't have to "be somebody" for the sake of your self-worth or self-esteem. Living with Christ as your sole identity will revolutionize the way you view yourself and others.

Those who are one with Jesus need not compare themselves with other people, resulting in either dreadful pride or debilitating inferiority. When you grasp the truth of your adoption in Christ, you'll see yourself as Abba sees you—as he sees his Son. And you'll share in the Son's deep sense of being loved, embraced and valued by the Father.

People everywhere are hungering for identity and belonging, love and acceptance. They long to fit in, to find themselves, to be liked and loved, yet many never truly discover what they're looking for.

If only they knew this gift freely given by God. If only they laid hold of union with his Son. If only they knew the security of heart that comes from living as Abba's child.

Imagine a child who, upon seeing her father, jumps for joy. With eyes lit up and a smile beaming from ear to ear, she runs to him as fast as her legs will carry her, calling at the top of her voice, "Papa! Papa!" She launches with reckless abandon into his outstretched arms, not once doubting he'll catch her. Hugging him as tightly as she can, she nestles into his tender embrace, enjoying the warmth of his loving presence. He holds her close and looks at her adoringly. Completely confident of the love and care that is hers in those arms, she whispers, "This is my safe place."

Of all God's gracious gifts to us in Christ, is there any sweeter than the gift of adoption?

8

The Greatest Love Story

"Do we live in God's brain, Daddy?" Téa asked as I drove her to school one day.

I chuckled at the imagery conjured up by my daughter's young mind. But as I considered Téa's question, I realized that what she seemed to be contemplating in her childlike simplicity was a biblical truth all adult Christians ponder at some point: the presence of God.

I gave my daughter an answer fit for her age. "Yes, Téa. We live in God's brain. God thinks about us all the time and he's all around us everywhere. He lives in your heart too, because you love Jesus."

She smiled, apparently liking that answer.

Here's an answer fit for adults.

Adopted into the Life of the Trinity

At the heart of God is love for others (Matthew 3:17; 17:5; John 3:35; 5:20; 10:17; 14:31; 17:24–26; Colossians 1:13). The Father loves the Son in the Spirit. The Son receives his

Father's love and reciprocates in the Spirit. And the Spirit is ever about this fellowship of mutual love.

Saint Bernard of Clairvaux expressed it endearingly: "If the Father is he who kisses, the Son he who is kissed, then see in the kiss the Holy Spirit, for he is… their unshakable bond, their undivided love, their indivisible unity."[16]

The heart of the Trinity is the giving and receiving of love. The Father, Son and Holy Spirit have eternally loved one another in a divine community of three persons. The Father and Son are forever focused upon each other in the Spirit, and in love they give to each other all they have. For "God is love" (1 John 4:8, 16).

Out of this relationship the whole cosmos was birthed and with it the pinnacle and crowning glory of creation: humanity. The Father, Son and Holy Spirit desired not to keep their life to themselves, but to selflessly share themselves and their love with human beings. In eternity past, God the Father was so in love with his Son in the Spirit that he wanted to share this love with many children, to draw them into his life and to embrace them with the very love he has for his Son.

And so, in love, God created the heavens and the earth and the animals and plants to serve as the environment for humanity, whom he made for relationship with himself.

When sin entered the world through Adam, the dynamic of humanity's relationship with God changed horrifically. The same love inspired the Trinity to act for our redemption so that God might once again welcome us into his life of fellowship and love. Only this time, the human experience of intimacy with God would be far greater than Adam and Eve could have ever dreamed. For the Son would unite humanity to himself, so that whoever believes in him could share in the life of the Trinity. In love, the Son was sent forth from the Father, in the power of the Spirit, to become fully human. To live, die and rise again so that in and through him the Spirit would lift us up into the loving fellowship of the Son with his Abba Father.

The Son of God stepped into human history to bring us true and eternal life. This is his promise: "I have come that you may have life and have it to the full" (John 10:10). Jesus gives us life—*his* life. He shares with us the very life of love and beauty, intimacy and joy, creativity and glory that he himself enjoys with the Father in the Spirit.

Christianity is the greatest love story ever.

"Come, join our dance, our celebration, our circle of love," God would say to each of us. We have been ushered into the inner life of the triune God (1 John 2:24).

The apostle Peter declared that this is "the best invitation we ever received!" Through Christ Jesus, we've been given "tickets to participation in the life of God" (2 Peter 1:3–4 MSG). We are "hidden with Christ in God" (Colossians 3:3).

Of all the privileges of grace, surely none is greater than this. "Our fellowship is with the Father and with his Son, Jesus Christ" (1 John 1:3). The Holy Spirit has taken us deep inside the heart of communion between the Father and Son, to participate in their shared life. As children of God, we exist in the Son and therefore in the continual presence of the triune God. Everything about us takes place in the community of the Trinity (2 Corinthians 13:14).

In Christ we don't go out from God's presence into the world; we go out into the world *in* God's presence.

Times of prayer, attending church and reading the Bible are not doorways that lead into God's presence, as if immediately prior we were without his presence. Prayer, church services and pondering Scripture are times of heightened awareness and experience of God's presence, when our words and thoughts are most consciously attentive to him. But our whole lives take place within the presence of the Father, Son and Holy Spirit.

Wherever you are and whatever you're doing—whether chatting with friends, going to work, mowing the lawn, feeding your baby—if you're a believer in Jesus, you live and move and have your being in the life and loving presence of the Trinity (Acts 17:28).

This is both comforting and empowering. Just as Jesus lived in his Father's presence (John 8:29), so we are never alone. If we're in Christ and he in us, and if Christ is in the Father and the Father in him, and if the Spirit is the bond of these two unions, then the triune God is with us always, to bless, lead and enable us (John 14:20, 23; 17:21, 23, 26). Jesus assured us, "I am with you always, to the very end of the age" (Matthew 28:20).

A dear friend of mine diagnosed with breast cancer was terrified about her surgery. As she lay in the preoperative room, she was suddenly comforted by an awareness that her life was hidden with Christ in God. She experienced a strong sense of Jesus's arms wrapped around her and of God the Father's arms around them both.

Encouraged in her faith and calmed by God's caring presence, she found her fear dissipated.

In her words, "I was at peace in Christ. I had hope for my present circumstance and of my promised eternal home in him."

Adopted in Christ as Abba's children and lifted up by the Spirit to share in the Son's communion with the Father, Christians are assured of one sublime thought above all others: We are loved more than we ever dare dream or hope.

Paul wrote:

> I am convinced that neither death nor life, neither angels nor demons, neither the present nor the future, nor any powers, neither height nor depth, nor anything else in all creation, will be able to separate us from the love of God that is in Christ Jesus our Lord. (Romans 8:38–39)

Children through the Cross

"See that daughter of mine?" the Father asks his angels. "Isn't she the most beautiful sight you've ever seen?" He turns. "See my son over there? Isn't he delightful?" He spreads his arms wide. "They're all so special to me. So precious. Enough to die for."

For our adoption to become possible, human sin had to be dealt with once for all. The Son came to earth, lived, died and rose again so that we might become Abba's children.

The writer of Hebrews tells us that God's ultimate goal for humanity is to "bring many sons and daughters to glory." And this he accomplished through the suffering and perfection of his own Son (Hebrews 2:10).

The sweetest part of all is that God has done it all and he gives it all to us by grace.

9

Sisyphus in the Church

n Greek mythology, Sisyphus was condemned by the gods to pointless labor. He had to roll a heavy boulder uphill, only to have it escape his grasp near the top and then watch it tumble back down to the valley below. Sisyphus was then forced to begin this burdensome struggle again, with the same outcome—repeatedly, forever. He'd been consigned to an eternity of futile effort as punishment for his crimes against the gods.[17]

The myth of Sisyphus is an illustration of the way many Christians live. Convinced that God has condemned them for their sins, they feel forced to strive in an uphill struggle to gain God's favor through good works, only to lose that favor the instant they sin next. Back in the valley of sin, they believe they must once again begin the onerous uphill struggle to re-earn God's love.

This useless attempt at self-salvation is commonly called Christian legalism.

God's Portrait

Over the centuries, the church has had a lot of misconceptions about God and his character. A common portrait of God is painted using the austere colors of a courtroom—depicting him as a cold, harsh, faceless judge who is angry with sinful humanity, yet appeased by the cross of Christ.

A more biblical portrait uses colors that accentuate the Father-heart of God. These vital colors produce a beautifully blended hue of love, grace and faithfulness.

Some Christians overlook the Father-heart of God because of poor church teaching. Others do so as the result of an unhealed father wound. Still others overlook God's Father-heart because of their own negative thinking. For many, it's a combination of these factors.

Regrettably, I've walked this path myself.

Striving for Grace

In my early Christian years, I believed that God condemned me when I sinned and blessed me when I was good.

In my mistaken belief, God was a stern judge who is easy to displease and quick to pass sentence whenever his holy law is broken. Every time I sinned, I believed God thundered judgment upon me. Down came the gavel. *Bang.* I felt God become distant, as if he'd turned his face away from me. I no longer sensed his loving embrace.

In those days, I dwelled on my sin and worried about what God thought of me. Even the smallest of petty sins troubled my conscience. I was forever confessing my sins and trying to make amends for them through good works, believing this to be necessary to get right with God again. I strived hard to get back into God's good graces.

Essentially, I was convinced that it was up to me to win God's mercy, favor and love. But all my legalistic efforts were in vain.

We can't bridge the sin-created gap between ourselves and God through self-effort. We can't work our way into Abba's lavish embrace. We can't earn our salvation. Trying to make ourselves right with God in our own strength is like trying to fly by flapping our arms really fast. We can no sooner save ourselves than we can teach an ant about quantum computing.

The Legalist's Error

Legalists confuse justification (our acceptance before God) with sanctification (our growth in holiness of life). They mistakenly believe that justification is dependent on sanctification and therefore attempt to be made right with God by living a holy life.

These people think they're making milestones toward God when in fact they're creating millstones around their necks. Legalism is a dreadful burden and highly destructive to one's spirituality. It destroys any hope of real joy, peace and assurance before God. No wonder legalists are prime candidates for spiritual burnout and disillusionment of faith.

To alleviate their burden, and their spiritual exhaustion, legalists develop coping mechanisms. They may compromise with certain forms of sin, which allows those sins to become common and habitual even while their struggle to overcome God's judgment continues. They turn a blind eye to their "lesser" sins—like white lies or gossip—but come down hard on themselves for sins they believe are more grievous to God.

This is lamentable because God is far more gracious than we give him credit for. We don't have to earn our standing with him in any way whatsoever.

10

Freedom

On Golgotha, a place called The Skull, soldiers thrust Jesus to the ground and stretched him out on a cross. He panted with exhaustion. His flesh was shredded from barbaric lashings. His face and body were bloodied and bruised from savage beatings. His skin seared as if on fire. Blood flowed from his thorn-punctured scalp.

As the hammer blow sounded, pain shot through Jesus's hand and arm. A loud groan of agony vented through his gritted teeth. His fingers contorted and quivered. Blood streamed from his nail-pierced palm onto the gnarled wood and dripped onto the dusty ground.

As the soldiers changed position to wrench his other arm straight, Jesus's panting quickened. More hammer blows fell at his other palm. He groaned again in anguish.

Then the soldiers moved to his feet. Intense pain took him to the brink of unconsciousness. As rusted metal scraped bone and pierced flesh, Jesus cast his eyes heavenward.

Finally the hammer blows ended. Jesus gazed into the merciless eyes of his slaughterers, his heart aflame with love for his tormentors. "Father, forgive them, for they do not know what they are doing" (Luke 23:34).

Sneering, the executioners spat on him and took his clothes.

The cross was raised to vertical, then dropped into a hole with a jolting thud. Jesus's body seized in excruciating pain. Breathing became even more difficult.

For hours, the beloved Son of God hung naked and disfigured on a wooden cross. The King of kings, mocked and taunted. The Lord of lords, despised and rejected. The Light and Life of the world, giving his life and light for all.

Darkness came over all the land like pitch-black night.

The Crucible

For Jesus, the physical and mental torment of being crucified was brutal beyond imagination, but the spiritual torment was far worse. In the cruelest way humanly possible, the sinless Son endured sin's penalty: spiritual death. All because of his love for the Father. And for us.

In perfect submission to his loving Father's will, Jesus offered himself as the ultimate sacrifice for the sins of human history. He died our death. He went to hell on our behalf, taking upon himself the punishment our sins deserve.

This was pure love.

The one who knew no sin took upon himself the weight of the world's sin and submitted himself to the judgment we deserve. Dying on a cross, he experienced a loss of conscious union with the Father. "My God, my God, why have you forsaken me?"

he cried in despair (Matthew 27:46). He experienced the loss of his Father's favor, exclusion from his Father's presence, and absence of participation in his Father's glory.

"It is finished," declared Jesus. "Father, into your hands I commit my spirit" (Luke 23:46; John 19:30).

With that, Jesus bowed his head and breathed his last. The incarnate Son of God was dead.

In that moment, sin and death triumphed. The demons of hell and Satan himself shrieked in victory. Those who loved Jesus crumpled to the ground and wept uncontrollably. The last of their hope was now extinguished.

Three days passed.

Then, just before dawn on the third day, the inconceivable happened. In life's greatest mystery, Jesus Christ rose from the dead. By the power of the Holy Spirit, the Father vindicated his Son. Sin, death and the devil were defeated.

"He is risen!" trumpeted the angels. The mountains sang, the waters danced, the trees clapped their hands in jubilation. The Way, the Truth and the Life was alive. The Light of the world shone brightly again. Humanity had been set free from their slavery to sin, law and death. Free from guilt and condemnation. Free from satanic and demonic authority.

His disciples could barely believe their ears and their eyes. Jesus showed them his hands and feet. Amazed, they worshiped him and laughed and cried in the joy of it all.

After appearing to his followers, the resurrected Christ ascended to his Father's right hand.

In our age of heightened individualism, it's easy to fall into the trap of believing that salvation is primarily our responsibility. It is not. God saves us—by grace, through faith, in Christ alone.

The Atonement

Since God's righteous judgment against sin barred our access to him, it was necessary that the Son obtain our reconciliation with God. Sent by the Father in love and grace, the Son stepped out of eternity and into the chaos and brokenness of human history to redeem and restore us.

From cradle to cross, Jesus fulfilled the law and all righteousness (Matthew 3:15; 5:17; Luke 2:40, 52; John 15:10). As a child, he was obedient in things to which children are tested. As an adult, he was obedient in things to which adults are tested. He spent his whole life perfecting our humanity and this accomplishment shone brightest in his death and resurrection. On the cross, sin was defeated once and for all— not merely our individual sins, but the foundation that lies beneath: the bedrock of Adam's original sin.

In his life and on the cross, Jesus banished our separation from God and reconciled us with him forever. This is the atonement. It's the center of the gospel and the heart of Christianity.

When my baby girl, Christelle, eats a meal, more food ends up on her face, hands and clothes than in her tummy. My wife and I, shaking our heads, use a washcloth to wipe her. In the process, the washcloth gets filthy. Before encountering Christelle, that cloth was pristine and perfect, spotless, without blemish. In order to clean Christelle, the cloth has to take her mess, making her filth its own, becoming soiled so that she might be made clean.

This is a picture of atonement. "God made him who had no sin to be sin for us, so that in him we might become the righteousness of God" (2 Corinthians 5:21). Jesus, the pure and perfect one, took our sin upon himself. He was made dirty for us. He bore the filth of our fallen condition so that sinners might be made clean, as pure and white as snow. He became sin so that we might be made holy and blameless, the righteousness of God, reflections of God's glory.

Love and Justice in Perfect Unity

When we view the cross of Christ, God may seem like an angry Father, bitterly punishing his Son for the sins of humanity. But that is a misrepresentation of God.

Yes, Jesus took the wrath of God upon himself at the cross. But the Father was not angry with his obedient, beloved Son—nor with humanity, whom he loves.

It's important for us to see the Father's heart in the cross. Jesus came as *God for us* (Ephesians 1:3–14). The Son came to save humanity from sin because the Father sent him (John 3:16–17). Jesus came to give us access to his Abba Father because that's what the Father wants for us (John 14:6; Hebrews 2:10).

The cross is all about the Father taking action through his Son by his Spirit to enter the deepest caverns of hell, to wrap his arms around a shackled humanity dead in sin and to hold them in his lavish embrace. He destroyed sin and death so absolutely and crushed evil and Satan so completely, that he shattered the chains that bind humanity. He set us free from our spiritual bondage by smashing hell's gates and bursting forth spectacularly from the abyss, lifting up a restored humanity in triumphant glory.

In the cross of Christ, God's love and mercy come together with his holiness and justice in perfect unity. Yes, God despised our sin. Yes, sin had to be dealt with and punishment served, for God is holy, righteous and just. But in Jesus, God lovingly and mercifully took upon himself our sin and punishment.

God doesn't love us only because Jesus died for us. Jesus died for us *because* God loves us (John 3:16; Ephesians 2:4–5; 1 John 4:10).

11

Forgiven

The hymn "It Is Well with My Soul" was written in 1873 by Horatio G. Spafford, a prominent lawyer, real estate investor and devout Presbyterian. This hymn, capable of evoking intense emotion, is made all the more compelling when we look at the great pain Spafford was enduring when he wrote it.

Two years before composing these lyrics, Horatio was brought to his knees financially when the Great Chicago Fire of 1871 swept through his city, destroying most of his sizable real estate fortune. A short time before this, he had experienced the death of his son. Seeking respite, Horatio decided to take his family to Europe.

Business commitments delayed Horatio's departure, so he sent his wife and four daughters on ahead of him. During their voyage across the Atlantic, in the predawn hours of November 22, 1873, their sailing ship collided with a Scottish sea vessel and sank. Horatio's wife survived, but all four daughters died, along with 222 other passengers.

Nine days later, when the survivors landed at Cardiff, Wales, Horatio's wife sent him a telegram, opening with "Saved alone."

On receiving the news, Horatio took to the seas to join his beloved. As his ship passed over the ocean depths where his four little girls had drowned, he was inspired to pen an impassioned hymn.[18]

Here are the first three of six verses:

> When peace, like a river, attendeth my way,
> When sorrows like sea billows roll,
> Whatever my lot, Thou hast taught me to say,
> It is well, it is well with my soul.

> Though Satan should buffet, though trials should come,
> Let this blest assurance control,
> That Christ hath regarded my helpless estate,
> And hath shed His own blood for my soul.

> My sin, oh, the bliss of this glorious thought,
> My sin, not in part but the whole,
> Is nailed to His cross, and I bear it no more;
> Praise the Lord, praise the Lord, O my soul!

How can a person who lost so much say, "It is well with my soul"?

Horatio understood the cross. He knew grace. He'd experienced forgiveness of sin and that brought peace and assurance to Horatio's soul, even amid life's cruelest tragedies and deepest sorrows.

Our Need of a Savior

Paul's letter to the Romans is arguably the most complete exposition of the gospel message ever penned. He devotes the first three chapters to the seriousness of sin and our need for a Savior.

In order to fully understand grace in Christ, we must first acknowledge our sin problem. Paul tells us, "There is no one righteous, not even one… All have sinned and fall short of the glory of God" (Romans 3:10, 23). We're all dead in sin and powerless to attain salvation ourselves. We desperately need a Savior.

Forgiven of All Sin

But Paul doesn't leave us wallowing in our sin. After identifying our sin problem, he fixes our eyes on Jesus.

Christ's work on the cross took away all our sin and now in Christ we are totally forgiven by God. He has forgiven all our sin—past, present and future.

God doesn't count our sins against us (2 Corinthians 5:19; Romans 4:6–8). He remembers them no more (Hebrews 8:12). Our original sin in Adam? Forgiven. Our sinful thoughts, attitudes, speech and action? Forgiven. Our sins of omission? Forgiven. Even those sins we fear might be unforgivable have been forgiven forever. As far as east is from west, that's how far the Father has cast our sin away from us (Psalm 103:8–13).

Many Christians, when they sin, run away from the Father. But Abba runs toward them with arms open wide, like a loving earthly father eager to welcome his prodigal child home (Luke 15:11–32).

There's no sin under the sun that can put us beyond the reach of God's love, grace and forgiveness. "In Christ we have redemption through his blood, the forgiveness of sins, in accordance with the riches of God's grace that he lavished on us" (Ephesians 1:7–8).

12

Positively Righteous

The moment you first believed in Jesus Christ as your personal Savior, the Father united you with his Son by his Spirit, forgave you of all sin and lavished upon you all the treasures of his Son (Ephesians 1:3).

One of the finest and most exquisite gems among these treasures is justification. By grace you are justified through faith in Jesus Christ. But what does *justification* mean?

A Gem of Great Worth

When I was a teenager, I was taught that being justified means "just-as-if-I'd never sinned." It's a playful memory aid, but a poor definition.

Why? Because justification is far more than forgiveness.

Think of it in terms of a bank account. Sin is debt—a massive debt, far too big to ever pay off. Forgiveness takes you from this negative balance to a zero balance. Your debt has been repaid. It's just as if you'd never sinned, which is fantastic beyond words.

But God has done abundantly more than simply cancel your debt. He's given you a limitless credit. God has given you the righteousness of Christ—Jesus's lifelong perfect obedience to the law and will of God. There's no upper limit on these riches of righteousness.

That is a picture of justification.

Justification is God's act of declaring us righteous on account of Christ's righteousness. Jesus the Righteous One is our righteousness for justification (1 Corinthians 1:30). We simply *must* be united with him in order to share in his righteousness (2 Corinthians 5:21; Romans 5:16–19).

We're made righteous in God's sight in Christ, and this, by grace, through faith (Romans 3:21–4:25; Ephesians 2:8–9). The purpose of faith is to unite us with Christ, in whom all the treasures of heaven are embodied.

When the Father looks upon you, he sees you as his perfectly righteous child because you are united with his perfectly righteous Son. He sees you as righteous, not because of anything you've done but because of everything Jesus is and has done for you. Your heavenly Father looks on you and says, "This child is in my Son, with whom I am well pleased."

Since you've been justified through faith, you have peace with God through Jesus Christ (Romans 5:1). In him, you may approach God with freedom and confidence (Ephesians 3:12). The doorway to his throne of grace has been thrown wide open by the blood of his Son (Hebrews 4:16; 10:19–22). "Come," God would say to each of us, "enjoy my loving presence."

"For through him we have access to the Father by one Spirit" (Ephesians 2:18).

In Christ, we've been made right with God. This is the gospel rest I now live in. We all can.

Having a Gospel Mindset

From the days of our childhood, we're taught by family and society that rewards come from good works. If I'm a good girl and eat my vegetables, Mommy will give me ice cream. If I've been a good boy, Santa will bring me presents. If I work hard for an employer, I'll be paid. It's the "if-then" language of law: If this, then that. If I obey God, he'll accept me.

The gospel turns this thinking on its head. It speaks the "because-therefore" language of grace: Because this, therefore that. Because Christ obeyed God, God accepts me.

We must take care not to bring the language of law into our relationship with God. For example, we should never think that grace got us into God's kingdom but now moral performance keeps us in it. Why would the Father save us through faith by grace when we were wretched sinners, only to make us retain our salvation by works once we're his precious children? That thinking is illogical and unbiblical. We don't save ourselves. God does (Ephesians 2:8–9).

We were saved by grace, we are being saved by grace, and we will be saved by grace. From start to finish, it's all an act of God's grace. "And if by grace, then it cannot be based on works; if it were, grace would no longer be grace" (Romans

11:6). Even our Christian living is a work of God in us, though we certainly play an active role in it (Philippians 2:12–13).

Where grace reigns, *being* always comes before *doing*. We're first a Christian, a child of God, by grace, and then we express it, whether well or poorly. We're first righteous by faith, and we're called to live in ways that are right. Sanctification flows out of justification, not the reverse. We're first pardoned in order to become holy; we aren't holy in order to be pardoned.

To believe that we have to *do* good works in order to *be* a Christian (or become more of a Christian) will leave us feeling insecure. If we think that righteousness before God is our responsibility, we'll be continually wondering if we're making the grade. Confessed my sins today? Check. Read my Bible today? Check. Prayed to God today? Check. Showed love today? Check. And for double reassurance: Went to church on Sunday? Tithed this week? Check, check. Good. I'm worthy of God's approval today.

No, no, no! Ten thousand times, no! "You foolish Galatians!" shouts the apostle Paul. "Who has bewitched you? Before your very eyes Jesus Christ was clearly portrayed as crucified… Are you so foolish? After beginning by means of the Spirit [that is, by grace though faith], are you now trying to finish by means of the flesh [that is, by law through self-effort]? Clearly no one who relies on the law is justified before God, because 'the righteous will live by faith'" (Galatians 3:1, 3, 11).

We are "not justified by the works of the law, but by faith in Jesus Christ" (Galatians 2:16). Our status before God isn't dependent on what we do but on what Christ has done.

Why would we ever think we need to do good deeds to please God? Is the Father not pleased with Jesus? Of course he is. So too, he's pleased with us who are one with his Son.

Yes, deeds are important. James 2:14–26 tells us that good works are the fruit and evidence of genuine faith. But they're not important for justification.

We should never look outside Jesus for our justification. Never have a "Jesus-plus" approach—Jesus plus our own works. As Paul insists in Galatians 2:21, if righteousness could be gained through our efforts, then Christ died for nothing.

Even if we wanted to get right with God through keeping his law, we would have to obey it perfectly, like Jesus did. And that's impossible (Galatians 2:16), because we all sin (Romans 3:23).

The penitent criminal hanging on a cross next to Jesus ought to be proof that we don't achieve salvation. He had no time to do things for God. No time to earn divine favor. No time to do anything except trust in Jesus. Yet Jesus told him, "Today you will be with me in paradise" (Luke 23:40–43).

In Christ, you are righteous in God's sight, despite your sin. As Martin Luther said, a Christian is "at the same time righteous and a sinner."[19] We don't have to get our act together for God to embrace us.

We mustn't rely on our superficial emotions—one day feeling favored by God, the next feeling distant from him. Emotions are never the gauge for measuring God's view of us. The only true gauge is Jesus.

13

Fear Is Gone

When you first came to faith, you were instantly united with Jesus in his death and resurrection. Paul tells us that "we died with Christ" (Romans 6:8), "we died to sin" (6:2), we've been "baptized into his death" (6:3) and "buried with him" (6:4). Note the past tense.

"If we have been united with him in a death like his, we will certainly also be united with him in a resurrection like his" (6:5). Note that the verb tense here is future in relation to our death with Christ. Paul isn't referring to the end-times resurrection of the body.[20] He is helping us see that we've already died, having shared in Jesus's death and resurrection, and now we're alive to God forevermore (6:11).

Died to Sin

Paul tells us Christ *died to sin*. That's an important phrase to understand.[21] "The death he died, he died to sin once for all" (Romans 6:10). This can mean only one thing for Jesus who knew no sin. Christ bore the penalty of sin, namely death.[22]

His death was "the wages of sin" (Romans 6:23). He took upon himself the judgment and punishment for our sin.

In Christ, we've died to sin (Romans 6:2, 11). We've gone through final judgment and punishment for sin before God.

The fact that Jesus died for us doesn't mean we escaped sin's penalty. We didn't bypass death or cheat it. We went through Christ's death by virtue of our union with him. And just as Christ was raised from the dead to newness of life, completely vindicated and justified from all sin, so too have we, in him (Romans 6:4–5, 10–11). The judgment of God and the penalty for our sin is now a thing of our past.

Paul urges us, "Count yourselves dead to sin but alive to God in Christ Jesus" (Romans 6:11). You have been set free from the kingdom of sin, death and darkness, and brought into the kingdom of grace, life and light (Romans 6:7; 2 Corinthians 5:17; Colossians 1:12–13). This happened to you at conversion and it's the meaning of your water baptism.

This truth is incredibly liberating. If you've died with Christ, then neither death nor sin can rule over you anymore. Sin has no power to hand you over to God's law for judgment. It can no longer condemn you to eternal death. Punishment for sin is behind you, in the past—and God will never bring it against you again (John 5:24).

We cannot go through judgment and death a second time. Just as Christ cannot die to sin again (Romans 6:9), neither can we (Romans 6:11).

So there's nothing to fear about what sin can bring us before God. Death has lost its sting (1 Corinthians 15:55–57).

We can rest assured that when we breathe our last and go to meet our Maker, he'll welcome us into eternal glory with open arms.

No Condemnation

There is no condemnation for those who are in Christ Jesus (Romans 8:1–2). We've been set free.

The next time the devil throws your sins in your face, accusing and condemning you, tell him, "Yes, I'm a sinner. Yes, I deserve death and hell. But I know and love the one who has conquered every sin. In Jesus I'm forgiven and righteous, and now I rest in the Father's loving embrace. So get lost, you putrid liar." [23]

As a Christian, you'll never be condemned by God for sin. However, you will be convicted of sin. Conviction comes from the Holy Spirit. It produces godly sorrow—the awareness of having grieved Abba's heart. Condemnation is of the devil. It produces fear that God might reject you or hurt you. Conviction is loving, gentle and tenderly firm. Condemnation is nagging and accusing. Conviction identifies a specific sin and the actions needed for godly change. Condemnation is generalized and vague and offers no help. Conviction points you to God's grace, inviting you to fellowship with him. Condemnation points you to God's wrath. Conviction reminds you of your peace, assurance and joy in Christ. Condemnation conjures up feelings of guilt, shame, insecurity and failure. Conviction seeks to build you up, transform you and give you hope.

Conviction is truth. Condemnation is a lie.

Remember that distinction every time you sin. It will encourage your faith in Christ.

If I wrong my spouse, I don't have to ask, "Are we still married?" If a child offends his parent, he is still the parent's child. When you sin, you don't need to ask, "Am I still God's child?" Of course you are.

Some might wonder, "If God has completely forgiven me, why does he bother to convict me when I sin? And why do I need to ask for forgiveness if I'm already forgiven?"

God convicts us and we confess our sin; not for the sake of our justification (we're already justified) but for our *experience* of justification and also for our *sanctification*.

We ask for God's forgiveness, but we need just as much to thank him for already forgiving and justifying us in Christ. We don't confess our sins to God in order to be forgiven. We confess because we know we're already forgiven.

Who would confess their sins to a holy and just God, with the power to damn us to hell, unless they were first assured of forgiveness in Christ? But if we know God no longer counts our sins against us (2 Corinthians 5:19), we can confess, repent and give thanks with confidence.

Confession of sin is our response to the revelation of God's forgiveness.

Conviction by the Spirit brings godly sorrow, and godly sorrow brings repentance (2 Corinthians 7:9–10). It leads to confession and to the changing of our thoughts, attitudes, and behavior.

All in all, judgment and death as consequences of sin are in our past. Therefore, there's now no condemnation in Christ Jesus.

14

The Call to Discipleship

If God has forgiven us of all our sin and there's no divine judgment when we sin, we can live as we please, right? Because God's grace covers me, I can party like there's no tomorrow. Since there's no condemnation in Christ, why not go on sinning?

Grace Abuse

Taking advantage of God's grace cheapens it. It ignores the fact that the gospel is as much about sanctification as justification.

Paul frequently encountered this misunderstanding of the gospel (Romans 3:5–8; 5:18–6:1). The perverse argument goes like this: The more I sin, the more opportunity grace has to shine. Therefore, we should wallow in sin so God's glory may increase.

Paul responds in Romans 6:2 with the most belligerent of Greek rhetoric: *Mē genoito*, which means "Absolutely not! God forbid! What a ghastly thought!"

In the subsequent twelve verses, Paul explains why such thinking is wrong. He says, in effect:

> Don't you know that you've died to sin? United with Christ, you've died the death he died and you've risen with him into newness of life. You're no longer a citizen of sin's country. That's your old world. You live in God's country now. The old is gone; the new is here.
>
> So how could you possibly consider living a life of sin anymore? It's inconceivable to go on living in sin, having died to sin and risen with Christ. Sinful living is the former lifestyle of the former you in your former world. And though it's not impossible for you to return to your previous life and live as though you were still in your sins, it's unthinkable that you would want to.
>
> Since you're now alive to God in Christ Jesus, don't live as though you are still a citizen of sin's country, with sin as your master and you its slave. Rather, offer yourself to God as one who lives in his country under his grace.

Grace delivers us *from* sin, not *to* sin. It liberates us from the wages and power of sin; it doesn't grant us the liberty to sin.

Think of it this way. Your life is a biography in two volumes. Volume 1 is your story before Christ. Volume 2 is your story in Christ. Volume 1 ended when you died to sin with Christ. Volume 2 began when you rose with Christ to new life. Now that you're living in Volume 2, why would you want to reopen Volume 1?[24]

Honest Reflection

But *you* wouldn't abuse God's grace, would you?

Have you ever heard the silent whisper of the devil saying, "Why not sin? Go on. It'll be okay. You're under grace. You know God will forgive you"?[25] Do you ever give in to sin, knowing you'll confess it and experience forgiveness later?

Too often we have a casual attitude toward God's moral law. We view many of his commands as optional.

But God's will is that we be both justified and sanctified (Romans 8:30; 1 Thessalonians 4:3). When temptation comes our way, we ought to respond like Paul, "God forbid! I'm one with Christ now. The old is gone; the new is here. How could I even consider returning to the old?"

Jesus Can't Be Torn in Two

Jesus is the Justified One (1 Timothy 3:16) *and* the Sanctified One (John 17:19). He is our righteousness *and* our sanctification (1 Corinthians 1:30).

When we received Christ through faith, his whole person took up residence within us. We have him in his entirety. We have all of his benefits.

We can't have Christ for justification but not for sanctification. If we try to separate justification and sanctification, it's as if we're tearing Christ in two.[26]

Freedom to Live

Justification and sanctification come together in our lives to produce a beautiful freedom.

If you've died and risen with Christ and are now living in Christ's sphere of existence, forgiven of all sin, viewed as righteous by God, accepted by him, and set free from all guilt, condemnation, judgment and penalty for sin, you're free to live with God in joy, peace and assurance. When you're free from fear of what God might do to you over sin, you're free to live a selfless life, pleasing to the Father, because there's nothing you need to do for yourself to secure your relationship with God. You can put all your energies into loving, enjoying and submitting to your Abba Father and loving, serving and caring for your fellow humans. As Jesus said, "Freely you have received; freely give" (Matthew 10:8).

If you're worried about your sin and you fear the judgment of God, believing you need to earn his approval, you'll always be doing things "for God" with a hidden agenda. Your focus will be getting yourself right with God.

But in Christ we can live like a joyful child whose heart's sole desire is to delight our Abba and bring him glory.

We're saved *by* grace, but we're saved *for* good works (Ephesians 2:8–10).

15

Glorifying God

Have you ever pondered, "Why am I here? What's my purpose in life?"

You're born and raised. You become an adult and get a job. You get married and have kids. Along the way you make friends, earn money and acquire possessions. You grow old and retire. Throughout the years you experience life's ups and downs. At some point, you come to faith in Jesus Christ. Then one day you die and go to heaven. In short, the sun rises, the sun sets and in between, you're a busy little bee. What's the point of it all?

The older I get, the more important this question is to me... and the more deeply I'm comforted by its answer in Christ.

Our Search for Meaning

Everybody desires meaning in life. We all need that special cause or great purpose that brings significance, value and fulfillment to our existence. It's a universal human need, essential for our well-being.

The problem is, all too often we search for life's purpose in the wrong places.

Most people see their purpose in things like career, wealth, family, social justice, political crusades, religious causes. They believe that through such things they can help make a difference and have a positive impact in their own lives and the lives of others. This makes them feel good about themselves and the situation they've influenced. It brings a sense of satisfaction.

These things may hold intrinsic value, but often they're self-inspired. In other words, life's purpose becomes whatever we deem it to be, based on our own ideology and values.

To discover life's true purpose, there's only one place to look—to the only human who lived life the way God intended. We must understand our purpose in view of our union with Jesus.

The Response of the Faithful Son

From newborn cry to life's last breath, Jesus lived for the Father. He rejoiced in his Father and in delighting the Father's heart. He experienced his Father's love and showed him love in return. Jesus led a life of true and proper worship, in the Spirit and in truth. He glorified the Father all the days of his life.

With the deepest of filial affection and devotion, the Son's whole being roared, "Father, I love you. Everything I do, I do for you" (see John 14:31). His desire was always to please the one who sent him (Mark 14:36; John 5:30; 8:29). Both as a young boy and as a grown man, Jesus spoke his Father's words because he listened only for his Father's voice. He always performed his Father's work because he looked only to what his Father was doing (Luke 2:40–52; John 5:19; 12:49; 14:10).

To live for the Father was Jesus's life, his bread and meat (John 4:34). In his every act, word, thought and feeling, Jesus demonstrated his love for his Father.

His was a life of worship. Through this worship, the Son accomplished his life's prime purpose: to glorify the Father (John 14:13; 17:1, 4).

Jesus fulfilled his Father's will to save humanity from sin, death and Satan. He forgave and accepted the worst of sinners. He embraced the despised and marginalized. He restored the broken and lifted the downtrodden. He fed

the hungry, healed the sick, freed the oppressed. He helped the helpless, defended the powerless and gave hope to the disenfranchised. Jesus came to serve and to give away his life for the sake of others. And whatever he did, he did for the Father's glory.

His was the life of sonship. A life of submission and obedience, through which God the Father was revealed and glorified (John 14:9; 17:4).

The Response of the Faithful Child

We were created for God's glory (Isaiah 43:6–7; Romans 11:36). God made us for relationship with himself, that we may enjoy intimate communion with him and glorify him forever. Glorifying God is the greatest purpose of life.

Jesus glorified God through worship and we're called to share in his worship (Romans 12:1; Hebrews 13:15–16; 1 Peter 4:11). Only Jesus can teach us how to live as sons and daughters whose life-meaning is to glorify the Father.

Christian worship is the natural outflow from our identity in Christ. It's the response of love and submission to our Abba Father for who he is and what he has done for us. It's expressed in the things we think and feel, say and do.

Worship involves both adoration and action. Here's how Jesus summed up the life of worship: "Love the Lord your God with all your heart and with all your soul and with all your mind" and "Love your neighbor as yourself" (Matthew 22:37–40). Worship is about lovingly serving God and others.

It's about both heart and hand. First the heart, then the hand. More the heart than the hand, but ever the two together.

Worship is about sonship, not morality; relationship, not duty; joy, not drudgery (John 15:10–11). It's about sharing in Jesus's life with the Father, not rigid obedience to a strict moral code. It's about the Son living his life through you, cultivating in you the fruit and gifts of the Spirit as he works with your desires and abilities, personality and attitudes, and experiences and perspectives to bring glory to his Father in heaven.

Our whole life is meant to be an act of worship. As Paul says, "Whatever you do, whether in word or deed, do it all in the name of the Lord Jesus, giving thanks to God the Father through him" (Colossians 3:17). "Whether you eat or drink or whatever you do, do it all for the glory of God" (1 Corinthians 10:31).

16

Life's Great War

We are at war.

Our enemy is the devil. His goal is to oppose the one true God and to deceive and destroy those who believe in Jesus Christ. Intent on leading us off our path in Christ, Satan tries all kinds of sinister schemes to thwart our worship and glorification of God. He accuses us, criticizes us, condemns us and persecutes us. But his most potent weapon is temptation.

Satan's power is in lies and deceit (Genesis 3:1–6; John 8:44). Day and night, he and his demonic hordes conspire against us, tempting us where we're most vulnerable, in an effort to lure us away from God.

With evil principalities and powers never ceasing to seduce and persuade us, how can we hope to obey God's law and bring him glory?

One thing is certain: We can't do it in our own strength.

Do-It-Yourself Christian Living

Before becoming Christians, we were ignorant of God's law. The devil tempted us, our flesh listened attentively and we sinned without batting an eyelash.

But in coming to Christ, we became alive to God's law and therefore conscious of our sin. Indeed, we would not have known what sin was had it not been for the law (Romans 7:7).

Christians know God's law; it's written on our hearts by the hand of God. Now when Satan tempts us, the Holy Spirit quickens our conscience and draws the sword of Scripture, clashing with the enemy's blade and exhorting us to respond with faithful sonship.

Yet we remain torn. Despite our desire to submit to our Father's will, when we try to obey him, our flesh comes in alive and kicking.

In fact, knowing God's law arouses the sinful passions of our flesh, stimulating us to break God's commandments. In the words of Mark Twain, "There is a charm about the forbidden that makes it unspeakably desirable."[27] Or as Paul says, "Sin found a way to pervert the command into a temptation, making a piece of 'forbidden fruit' out of it. The law code, instead of being used to guide me, was used to seduce me" (Romans 7:8 MSG).

Listen to the apostle Paul's description of this inner struggle in Romans 7:

> What I don't understand about myself is that I decide one way, but then I act another, doing things

I absolutely despise. So if I can't be trusted to figure out what is best for myself and then do it, it becomes obvious that God's command is necessary.

But I need something *more!* For if I know the law but still can't keep it, and if the power of sin within me keeps sabotaging my best intentions, I obviously need help! I realize that I don't have what it takes. I can will it, but I can't *do* it. I decide to do good, but I don't really do it; I decide not to do bad, but then I do it anyway. My decisions, such as they are, don't result in actions. Something has gone wrong deep within me and gets the better of me every time.

It happens so regularly that it's predictable. The moment I decide to do good, sin is there to trip me up. I truly delight in God's commands, but it's pretty obvious that not all of me joins in that delight. Parts of me covertly rebel, and just when I least expect it, they take charge.

I've tried everything and nothing helps. I'm at the end of my rope. (Romans 7:15–24 MSG)

Paul may be referring to his days as a devout Jew, or perhaps his early Christian experiences while still piecing together in his own mind God's revelation in Christ for Christian living. Whatever the case, he clearly loved God and his law, but struggled to submit and obey.

Paul knew what it meant to experience inner conflict. He could relate to our frustration of having godly desires but being unable to carry them out. But when God revealed to him the truth about Christian living, he eagerly sought to explain it to us.

Although God's law is holy and right and good (Romans 7:12), and is our guide for life (7:7), simply knowing God's law isn't enough to overcome sinfulness. The law reveals and exposes sin, and even provokes us to sin, but it cannot rid us of sin. The law points to righteousness and holiness, but it cannot produce them in us.

All too often, we fall into the same trap Paul did initially: do-it-yourself Christian living. But even if we know the will of God, love it and want to do it, we cannot obey it in our own strength. We need something more.

The answer, Paul declares triumphantly, is Jesus:

> Is there no one who can do anything for me? Isn't that the real question?
>
> The answer, thank God, is that Jesus Christ can and does. He acted to set things right in this life of contradictions where I want to serve God with all my heart and mind, but am pulled by the influence of sin to do something totally different. (Romans 7:24–25 MSG)

God gave us the law to show us our sin in order to drive us continually into the arms of Jesus. As Paul says in Romans 8:1–17, in Christ and through him we are justified and sanctified. We worship and glorify our Abba Father by the indwelling Spirit, who unites us to Christ and shares with us Christ's life of sonship. The sanctified life is having Christ live out his filial life in us and through us.

A Work of God from First to Last

In an age dominated by radical individualism, it's easy to assume that our life of sanctification is an obligation we must fulfill. "I must worship and glorify God," people say, pushing on in their own strength.

Of course, worshiping and glorifying God *is* our responsibility, to a degree. We ought not sit back passively and expect God to do everything.

Therein lies the paradox of Christian living. Our dependence on God in Christ doesn't preclude our effort, and our working doesn't contradict his grace. In Paul's words: "Continue to work out your salvation with fear and trembling, for it is God who works in you to will and to act in order to fulfill his good purpose" (Philippians 2:12–13).

Paul doesn't say we cooperate with God or work alongside him, or that God does his bit and we pick up the rest. He doesn't say Christian living is a fifty-fifty partnership with God. Paul says we work out our salvation *because* God is at work in us. Sanctification is 100 percent the activity of God and 100 percent our activity.

Sanctification is a work of God's grace (1 Corinthians 1:30; Ephesians 2:8–10; 2 Timothy 1:9). God began a good work in us, and he'll carry it on to completion (Philippians 1:6). Grace doesn't end with forgiveness and justification, but carries into our Christian life of worship and beyond into our final glorification. It's all a work of God, from first to last (Romans 8:29–30).

Attitude of Gratitude

A popular way that Christians try to link grace and Christian living is through an "attitude of gratitude." In light of all the wondrous things God has done for us through Christ Jesus our Lord, we should show our thankfulness by responding with love and obedience. We live the life of worship because we're eternally grateful to God for saving us.

There's much to like about this attitude. Having gratitude to God is a beautiful, sincere, and essential Christian affection.

A common misunderstanding with the "attitude of gratitude" is that the gospel of salvation tends to be seen almost exclusively in terms of forgiveness and justification. If that's our thinking, we could easily come to believe that forgiveness and justification are what God does, while worship and sanctification are what we do. This bottles up grace completely in God's past work in Christ, leaving it up to our efforts to live the Christian life.

But even when gratitude to God is well understood, should gratitude be our main inspiration for the life of worship?

According to theologian John Piper, having gratitude as the primary motivation for Christian living is biblically unfounded. Yet in today's church, it is almost universally taught as the driving force in Christian living.[28]

Gratitude should be a secondary driver of worship, not the primary one.

We need a more biblical view of Christian living. We must see it through the lens of union with Christ.

17

Living Christ's Life

In my early Christian years, I believed Christian living amounted to three things: imitation, motivation and divine help.

I was sure I needed to imitate Jesus—to live like him and emulate his holy life. That's the gist of the Christian slogan of the 1990s: "What would Jesus do?"

I was also to have gratitude to God.

And I was to look to God for help.

There's nothing inherently wrong with these beliefs. We should uphold them. But I've since come to realize there's a better way. The primary driving force in Christian living should be our union with Christ.

Living by Grace

Jesus has not only taken our place in dying for our sin, but also in living out for us our life of worship.

The Christian life was first worked out and perfected in Jesus. Now, by virtue of our union with him, that life is communicated to us by the Holy Spirit. The Spirit crafts in us Christ's life of sonship that he lived on earth. Dwelling in us by the Spirit, Jesus transforms us from the inside out (John 15:5; Romans 8:9–11; 15:18; 2 Corinthians 13:5; Galatians 2:20).

Jesus shares his resources with us. He shares his trust in his loving Father and his desire to please him through loving obedience. He shares his sensitivity to the Spirit, that we might know where the Father is working. He shares with us his mind, his heart and his fruit and gifts of the Spirit. He shares his wisdom, ministry and prayers, his sufferings, strength and authority, his resurrection power, victory and rest, his hope and contentment, his entire life.

Hudson Taylor, a nineteenth-century missionary, called this "living the exchanged life." In a letter from China to his sister Amelia Broomhall in England, Hudson divulged his longtime struggle to become more like Jesus.[29] Excitedly, he

told Amelia about a newfound revelation that had helped him greatly in his pursuit of holiness: "resting on the Faithful One."

Jesus has done for us what we could never do. He faithfully obeyed the Father's will. United with him, we share in his faithful response. "[Christ's] resources are mine," wrote Hudson, "for *he* is mine and is with me and dwells in me. All this springs from the believer's oneness with Christ."

We don't show forth Christ's love by imitating his example, but through participation in his love. Our love for the Father is Christ's love for his Father. Our love for people is his love for humanity. And so we would say:

> If I have *agapē* love—divine, unconditional, self-sacrificing love—it's not mine; it's my Lord's. It is Jesus living in me, loving through me. In the same way, if I have gratitude to God, it is the Son's thankfulness to Abba. If I act with kindness, I act with his kindness.
>
> Whatever I need for life and worship derives from Jesus. If I need faith, I'll find it in Jesus's trust in the Father. If I seek patience, it lies in his forbearance. My sympathy, empathy and care for others is found in his compassion; my generosity and hospitality, in his self-giving; my joy, in Jesus's joy in the Father.

Any godliness we show is not ultimately ours but Christ's (Ephesians 2:10). As Jesus said, "For them I sanctify myself, that they too may be truly sanctified" (John 17:19).

This is the way to bring Christ into our home life, prayer life, workplace and friendships. It's how to live by the Spirit when we're helping others, resisting temptation, or serving in church. It's the way we can glorify the Father while hosting a dinner party, writing a report, or washing dishes.

Union with Christ is the key to a biblical understanding of discipleship. It's a matter of believing, with the apostle Paul, that "it is no longer I who live, but Christ who lives in me" (Galatians 2:20). All of life is meant to be lived in conscious communion with Jesus. As Paul instructs, "Just as you received Christ Jesus as Lord, continue to live your lives in him, rooted and built up in him" (Colossians 2:6–7).

If you're struggling to pray or to read your Bible, ask Jesus to teach you how the Father taught him to pray (Matthew 6:9–13) or what the Scriptures mean to him (Luke 24:27; John 5:39). In times of weakness, call on Jesus to strengthen you with the power by which his Father strengthened him (Luke 22:43; 2 Corinthians 12:9). If you experience rejection, desertion, or betrayal, pray for the love Jesus showed to those who abandoned him (John 13:1–14:3; see also Matthew 26:47–56, 69–75; 28:16–20; John 21:15–17). If you experience abuse or injustice, ask Jesus to share with you his power to forgive those who slaughtered him (Luke 23:34). In all circumstances, the Christian life is about sharing in the life of Jesus (Romans 8:28–29).

A friend of mine recently attended a film launch. While conversing with some colleagues, he noticed a man standing alone. After excusing himself, he walked over to the loner. The man shared about a deep trauma of his life. My friend told him his own story of isolation and misery that led him to meet Jesus.

What moved my friend to leave his comfort zone and share his testimony with a stranger? In his words, "The Spirit of Jesus. The one who can't bear to see anyone outside of his Father's loving embrace."

Another friend who is a Christian leader opened up about his past pornography addiction. He'd tried hard to resist the temptation, but usually gave in to it. This sin was devouring him on the inside and was harming his life and relationships (see James 1:15). Without self-restraint, he knew he was like a city that's been broken into and no longer has walls of protection (Proverbs 25:28).

Once my friend learned that his relationship with Christ allowed him to participate in the life of Jesus, he prayed daily for the self-control of Christ. He understood this fruit of the Spirit (Galatians 5:22–23) is a share in the discipline Jesus himself exhibited (Matthew 4:1–2; Hebrews 4:15). As he experienced the power of his union with Christ, he gradually overcame his struggle with pornography.

When you're tempted to sin, cling to Jesus. We're helped in times of temptation not by looking to the example of Jesus in his temptations and trying to copy him, but by virtue of his dwelling in us. The one who was tempted in every way and prevailed every time lives within you.

Jesus said, "I am the vine, you are the branches; he who abides in me and I in him, he bears much fruit, for apart from me you can do nothing" (John 15:5 NASB). We bear the fruit, but Jesus produces it. He shares his fruit with us. He's like a tree that's always green and flourishing and all our fruit comes from him (Hosea 14:8; 1 Chronicles

29:14). This fruit, cultivated in us for others to enjoy, tastes delectably divine to all who taste it.

That truth is incredibly liberating. United with Christ, we don't have to strive to worship God in our own strength. Jesus gives us his resources for living. We can rest in his faithfulness. The Christian journey "is not a burdensome trudge up a lonely road; it is a way that cuts through Jesus Christ himself."[30]

John Stott wrote, "The secret is not imitation (Christians imitating Christ's life) so much as reproduction (Christ reproducing his life through us)."[31] Or, as Hudson Taylor put it, "Do not let us consider him as afar off, when God has made us *one with him*... The only power for deliverance from sin or for true service is CHRIST." Living the Christian life has everything to do with "Christ in you, the hope of glory" (Colossians 1:27).

Dying and Rising with Christ

The blessing of being united with Jesus in his life of sonship comes with a cost because we're united to a crucified Savior.

The cross cast a shadow over Jesus's entire life. It loomed over him from the very beginning. His whole journey foreshadowed his future crucifixion. His was a selfless, sacrificial life. He continually died to his own will and submitted to his Father's. He was tested and afflicted for the sake of his Father and fellow humanity.

But through his sufferings Jesus was matured and perfected. Through humility and hardship came victory and glory. Through death came resurrection.

United with Christ, we have the power of the cross in our lives. We're called to a continual process of dying and rising with Christ. We're to take up our cross daily and follow Jesus, denying our own will in favor of the Father's (Luke 9:23–24). Putting to death our sinful nature and embracing the things of Christ (Colossians 3:1–17).

When we share in the sufferings of Christ, his resurrection power is always at hand for breakthrough and transformation (Philippians 3:10).

Faith in Action

Our life of worship is a gracious work of God in our lives. As the writer of Hebrews says, "May the God of peace… equip you with everything good for doing his will, and may he work in us what is pleasing to him, through Jesus Christ" (Hebrews 13:20–21).

This doesn't mean we become more like Jesus by osmosis. We aren't mere puppets of God in the theater of life. Living the life of sonship is about faith in action.

We work out our own salvation, but this is possible only because God works in us, supplying all we need through Christ's abundance (Philippians 2:12–13; 4:19). As Paul says of his labor for God's kingdom and glory, "To this end I strenuously contend with all the energy Christ so powerfully works in me" (Colossians 1:29). This is how we balance the paradox of absolute dependence on God and our effort, equally upholding our labor without contradicting his grace.

18

Life in the Spirit

As I write this book, I have three children under seven. I love them to bits. But gee, they know how to test my patience. Prayers that often pass my lips are "Lord, help me! Give me strength. Give me patience." If you're a parent, you know what I'm talking about.

But what do we mean when we ask God for help?

God's Help

Some Christians emphasize the role of the Holy Spirit in Christian living: "God empowers me by his Spirit." Others emphasize Jesus: "God strengthens me through Christ." Still others look simply to God: "God helps me."

But God is a Trinity and the Father, Son and Spirit always work together as one.

Yes, the Holy Spirit enables our Christian living, but what we receive from the Spirit isn't some vague influence or ethereal power. The Spirit never comes to us apart from Christ. The Spirit receives from Jesus what he gives to us

(John 15:26; 16:14–15; Romans 8:9–11; Ephesians 3:16–17; 6:17). For example, the fruit and gifts of the Spirit (Galatians 5:22–23; 1 Corinthians 12:1–11) are Christ's virtues and giftings, communicated to us by the Holy Spirit. Any talk of the Spirit's work in our lives must point to Jesus's own story, particularly his death and resurrection. The Spirit was given to share with us the Son's life with Abba (Romans 8:14–16) and to conform us to the Son's image (Romans 8:10–11, 29), crucifying our flesh and imparting to us the resurrection life of Jesus (Romans 8:13).

Jesus is the fount from which to draw all things for Christian living, but Jesus comes to us by the Holy Spirit. Without the Spirit, it's impossible for us to drink from the fountain of Christ (Romans 8:9–11; Ephesians 3:16–17).

The Holy Spirit makes Christ truly present in us. The Spirit takes Jesus Christ out of history and heavenly exaltation and brings him to us, to live in us and through us in our daily life. Whatever Christ gives to us out of his wellspring, he gives by the Spirit.

The Spirit and the Son work together to bring us everything belonging to the Son. And all that the Son gives to us by the Spirit is from the Father (John 16:15), to the glory of the Father (John 14:13).

When we ask God to help us, whatever the Father gives us is from the treasure trove of Jesus, given by his Holy Spirit.

Transformed by Trinitarian Grace

When I feel myself beginning to lose my temper with my three little rascals and I pray for patience, I'm asking the Father to give me the patience Jesus displayed when he walked this earth. I want Jesus to live his patience in and through me by the Spirit. I trust the Spirit to replicate the patience of Christ in me, for the Father's glory.

A pastor friend of mine who prays daily for a deeper share in the life and resources of Jesus described his experience of union with Christ this way:

> Over the years I have become increasingly conscious of inner drives that cannot possibly have their origin in me. When I sense a strong impulse to be generous, humble, or loving, this must be the work of the indwelling Spirit of Christ. My patience is a share in the "perfect patience" of Jesus (1 Timothy 1:16). My humility is a sign of "the mind of Christ" (Philippians 2:1–5). My experience of peace is the fulfillment of Christ's promise, "My peace I give to you" (John 14:27).

In the words of John Stott:

> It is no good giving me a play like *Hamlet* or *King Lear* and telling me to write a new play just like it. Shakespeare could do it; I can't. And it is no good showing me a life like the life of Jesus and telling me to live a life just like it. Jesus could do it; I can't. But if the genius of Shakespeare

could come and live inside me, I would then be able to write plays like he did. And if the Spirit of Jesus could come and live inside me, I would then be able to live a life like he did. This is the open secret of how to live as a Christian. It is not about us struggling in vain to become more like Jesus, but about allowing him, by the power of his Spirit, to come and change us from the inside.[32]

What a beautiful way to live!

Why Aren't We Perfect?

If the indwelling Spirit repeats in us the life of Jesus, and if Jesus indwells us to live in us and through us, why aren't we perfect? Why do we still struggle with sin?

There are several possible reasons.

First, from a historical perspective, we're in the time between Christ's first and second comings. The fullness of Christ is ours now, yet we won't completely experience that fullness until the age to come.

Second, our faith is weak. We don't even have faith the size of a mustard seed (Matthew 17:20).

Third, the struggles that take place in our lives, and the accompanying victories, bring God glory.

Last, we're dealing with a mystery. Only God knows why he designed sanctification to be progressive. His ways are higher than our ways (Isaiah 55:8–9) and he has good purposes in all his plans. We must accept this mystery by faith.

Similarly, while one person may pray for Christ's healing power and then experience a physical miraculous healing, ten other people may pray the same thing, in the same way, and not get the answer they hope for. We must trust that God knows best.

We are God's workmanship (Ephesians 2:10). We're called to remain sensitive to the Spirit's promptings, to recognize that God sets the timing of our sanctification and glorification and to trust him to lead us ever deeper into the life of his Son.

Heart, Not Perfection

God isn't looking for sinless perfection from us in this life. He's interested in our hearts.

King David is revered in Scripture as "a man after God's own heart," even though his sins were considerable (1 Samuel 13:14; Acts 13:22; compare 2 Samuel 11:1–27).

None of us will reach perfection this side of heaven. We mess up all the time. But over time our lives will show less of us and more of Christ as we prayerfully seek by faith to share in his resources by the Spirit.

We're still on the journey; we haven't reached the end. And though Jesus walked this path perfectly for us and now shares his all with us, our life isn't about perfection. It's about growing in Christ.

We have an Abba Father who is so gracious that he accepts our imperfections. He cherishes hearts that yearn for him.

19

United We Stand

Now that we've examined the nature of our personal relationship with God, I'd like to broaden our horizons and look at a bigger picture: our union with Christ in light of church and ministry. By *church* I mean the body of all believers bonded together in Christ. By *ministry* I mean the ongoing outpouring of Christ to his church and through her to the whole world. It's a work to which all believers have been called, not just ordained pastors or clergy.

Smoking Coals and Lone Rangers

Remember the excitement you felt when you first gave your heart to Jesus? The gospel was a soothing balm for your troubled soul. The Bible shone into your life like the morning sun dispelling the night. Prayer felt life-giving. The Lord's Supper inspired you. The pastor's sermons were like music to your ears. Songs of worship touched you deeply. Christian friendships added fresh vigor to your week. You smiled every time you thought about Jesus.

But time, as well as some experiences of your Christian journey, may have made your walk with the Lord lose some of its shine. The elation of a new convert doesn't last forever. Like a child's euphoria on Christmas morn, it eventually ebbs away. You still believe in Jesus, but perhaps your enthusiasm for church has faded. You continue going to church, but out of duty or guilt more than passion. You mumble a few songs, drift in and out of the sermon, then catch up with friends over coffee before heading home. You used to be on fire for God, but now you feel more like a smoking coal.

Others, disillusioned with church, become lone rangers. They don't feel a need for church because they don't get anything out of it. "Besides," they say, "too many hypocrites go there." Perhaps they got hurt a few years ago, so now they prefer online sermons and on-demand worship music.

In our age of heightened individualism, it's easy to get caught up in the self-centeredness and selfishness of the world. We convince ourselves that the church exists to serve our needs. When the church fails to serve us, we lose interest or we toss it aside. Or worse, we experience a crisis of faith.

In Need of a Fresh Vision

We need a fresh vision of church based on the early church described in the book of Acts. Those pioneers of the faith understood two things with clarity: the church as the body of Christ, and the heart of church life as *koinonia*.

A Tapestry of Astonishing Beauty

The church isn't "song and sermon" or "meetings and meals" or flashy new programs. Nor is she ornate cathedral ceilings or concert-like settings. She isn't a building or denomination, nor an organization or institution. The church is a living organism, a local and worldwide community of believers in collective union with their Lord.

Listen to Jesus's astounding prayer about us:

> I pray… that all of them may be one, Father, just as you are in me and I am in you. May they also be in us so that the world may believe that you have sent me. I have given them the glory that you gave me, that they may be one as we are one—I in them and you in me—so that they may be brought to complete unity… I have made you known to them and will continue to make you known in order that the love you have for me may be in them and that I myself may be in them (John 17:20–23, 26).

We, the children of God, are a body of people not bound by the limits of culture, personal spiritual preference, or even time in history, but one through union with Jesus Christ by the Holy Spirit. We're a single community in Christ, despite our differences in style and spirituality, theology and themes, lingo and liturgy. We're made up of every race and nation, every tribe and tongue, woven together into a tapestry of many colors and astonishing beauty.

We are, as Paul said, the body of Christ (Romans 12:4–5; 1 Corinthians 12:27; Ephesians 1:22–23; 4:15–16; 5:23, 30). United with Christ, our head, we are his body, joined and held together in him, growing together as one, with each part doing its work in total dependence on him. We're all, as C. S. Lewis says, "organs" of Christ's body.[33]

Life in union with Christ is personal, but it is also ecclesiastical. The truth of "Christ in us and us in Christ" has both an individual dimension and a corporate dimension. "For we were all baptized by one Spirit so as to form one body" (1 Corinthians 12:12–13).

Paul's first encounter with Jesus is richly illuminating:

> As he neared Damascus on his journey, suddenly a light from heaven flashed around him. He fell to the ground and heard a voice say to him, "Saul, Saul, why do you persecute me?"
> "Who are you, Lord?" Saul asked.
> "I am Jesus, whom you are persecuting," he replied.
> (Acts 9:3–5)

On the road to Damascus, Paul (known then as Saul) received one of his greatest revelations, one that would shape his theology forever: To cause pain to the church is to cause pain to Christ. Christ and the church are indissolubly one.

Jesus is united with us, his earthly church. And we are joined to one another in him. "There is neither Jew nor Gentile, neither slave nor free, nor is there male and female, for you are all one in Christ Jesus" (Galatians 3:28).

Our corporate union with Christ is ultimately experienced in our coming together to partake of Holy Communion. Whether you view this sacrament as symbolic or containing metaphysical significance, the Lord's Supper is a special occasion for deepened communion with Jesus. Through it the Spirit testifies to our spirits that we are personally one with Christ and together one body in Christ; that our faith may be strengthened both individually and collectively.

There's no such thing as a solitary Christian. Lone rangers misunderstand the intention of the Father, Son and Holy Spirit for humanity. The triune God designed the body of believers in his own image as a community engaging in intimate, loving fellowship.

The Christian life is lived in connection with others and for others, especially our brothers and sisters in Christ (Galatians 6:10).

Christians need one another. God meant for us to do life together. Without regularly receiving the preaching of the Word, the sacraments, the ministry of prayer and fellowship with other believers, there's a limit to Christian maturity.

Koinonia, Not Consumer

Many Christians go to church with the focus on "What can I get out of this?" For example, many enter into a time of praise and worship on Sunday mornings with the mindset that the most important thing about singing to the Lord is that it makes them feel better. Of course we're there to glorify God, but if we don't have some sort of spiritual high, we may feel let down… or think there was something wrong with the worship team.

Our measure of a church service becomes how much the song, sermon and sacraments move us personally. We say, "Wasn't that a great service?" if we felt uplifted by it, giving little thought to what God might have been doing in the service at large.

This consumer mentality is a product of the world we live in. But God never intended us to be consumers of church. It's not about what I can get, but what I can give—to God and to my brothers and sisters in Christ. We need to grasp the truth of *koinonia*.

Koinonia is a Greek word used in the New Testament to convey the idea of Christian fellowship, sharing and intimacy. It implies a mutual bond, a sense of unity of being and of purpose in our mission. Ultimately, it means having a common share in the life of Christ. *Koinonia* is not a passive word. It implies action. It signifies both being together and acting together, of mutual support for mutual benefit. It speaks of genuine interdependence.

Koinonia is the practical expression of union with Christ among believers. We're to live out, with one heart, the life of Jesus together.

At its heart is sonship. If we know God as our Abba Father and experience life in the Son, we'll understand what it is to be part of God's family.

True Christian fellowship isn't about idle chit-chat over coffee and donuts. It's about sharing together in Christ. It's about believers coming together and seeking to share Christ's life and ministry with one another (1 John 3:16). They gather regularly for meaningful conversation, committed prayer, studying Scripture and ministering love. They draw closer to the Father, Son and Holy Spirit in collective worship, thereby creating deep bonds with each other (Acts 2:42–47; 4:32–35; 20:35).

Christian fellowship involves being vulnerable and humble enough to share our real selves—our joys and hurts, strengths and weaknesses—without being judged. When others bare their souls, we're sensitive to the Spirit's promptings. There will be tears and celebration and deep inner healing when brothers and sisters stand together in unity and come alongside one another to support, comfort and encourage, with much intercessory prayer. We're a close-knit community, connected by faith in Christ.

Koinonia calls on every believer to contribute to the life of the church. We all share in Christ's life and his ongoing ministry. We display the fruit of the Spirit and the gifts of the Spirit as a blessing to our Christian family.

Exercising Our Giftedness

The Holy Spirit gives each of us one or more spiritual gifts, distributed as he determines. These gifts are to be used for the benefit of others. Spiritual gifts exist for the good of the whole Christian community (1 Corinthians 12:4–7).

It's incumbent upon us to know what part of Christ's body God has made us to be and to do the work of that particular part (Romans 12:4–8; 1 Corinthians 12:1–31; Ephesians 4:16). As Peter says, "Each of you should use whatever gift you have received to serve others, as faithful stewards of God's grace in its various forms" (1 Peter 4:10).

Exercising our gift will likely involve humbling ourselves and submitting to the repeated promptings of the Spirit. We may need to act by faith against our fear of rejection. Whatever the case, may we obediently release our gift for the sake of Christ's body, that Jesus might minister to our brothers and sisters through us.

Triple-Braided Cord

Koinonia binds us together and makes us stronger. We become like a cord of three strands that's not easily broken (Ecclesiastes 4:12). When our priority is our brothers and sisters in Christ, when we exhibit the fruit of the Spirit and exercise our spiritual gifts in love and humility, all are nurtured, nourished and built up in the faith (Romans 15:1–3; 1 Corinthians 12:1–11; 14:26). This is God's family in action. When God's children live like this, lives are transformed.

A close friend of mine was recently diagnosed with prostate cancer and underwent surgery. He experienced profound grief at the sudden, very real possibility of death, as well as deep heartache at the great sadness this would cause to his loved ones. It was a dark night of the soul. Yet with joy-filled tears he described God's answer to his prayers for strength.

"I've been greatly comforted and humbled by the outpouring of love, generosity and kindness from my Christian family," he told me. "What peace it's brought to my heart. Truly, Jesus has ministered to me through his church."

Koinonia is as simple and as difficult as this:

> In your relationships with one another, have the same mindset as Christ Jesus. (Philippians 2:5)
>
> If you have any encouragement from being united with Christ, if any comfort from his love, if any common sharing in the Spirit, if any tenderness and compassion, then... be like-minded, having the same love, being one in spirit and of one mind. Do nothing out of selfish ambition or vain conceit. Rather, in humility, value others above yourselves, not looking to your own interests but each of you to the interests of the others. (Philippians 2:1–4)

Koinonia bears the unmistakable fingerprints of Jesus.

Koinonia, Tiffs and Rifts

The church is a fascinating blend of men, women and children of all ages and backgrounds. This can be challenging. Personalities will clash. There'll be differences and disagreements. The rifts between Paul and Peter (Galatians 2:11–14) and Paul and Barnabas (Acts 15:36–41) are proof that church life isn't always harmonious, despite the Lord's desire for peace among us (Mark 9:50; Romans 14:19; Ephesians 4:3; Colossians 3:15; Hebrews 12:14). Christians are an eclectic bunch of redeemed sinners, a body of great diversity.

When tiffs are brewing, we'd do well to keep two things in mind.

First, God uses difficult people to mature us. "As iron sharpens iron, so one person sharpens another" (Proverbs 27:17). Humbly examine yourself. Take responsibility for your part in any conflict (Matthew 7:3–5) and seek to respond with Christlikeness.

Second, we're not all called to be of one personality or preference. God has woven great variety into his church. The oneness we're called to is that of one faith, one body, one purpose and one character—that of Christ.

Christian unity is an outflow of union with Christ. The glorious unity of the church comes from believers sharing in the life of Jesus. Empowered by the Spirit, they radiate his life into one another's lives, each in their own unique way.

Koinonia is about unity, not uniformity. Harmony, not division (1 Corinthians 1:10). "How good and pleasant it is when God's people live together in unity" (Psalm 133:1).

The Great Commission

From this place of God-breathed family fellowship, the church goes out into all the world to fulfill the Great Commission.

Our vision and ministry should never be limited to the four walls of a church building. It must spill out into every arena of society. We're called first and foremost to lovingly attend to the needs of those who belong to the family of believers (Galatians 6:10). Yet the church exists for the world, not for itself. We have a transforming mission: to be witnesses to God and his kingdom through participation in Christ's ongoing ministry to the nations (Matthew 28:19–20).

20

Kingdom Ministry

In the opening verse of the book of Acts, Luke draws our attention to "all that Jesus began to do and to teach," as chronicled in Luke's "former book," which we know as the Gospel of Luke. I'm intrigued by Luke's word choice: "all that Jesus *began* to do and to teach." This implies that Jesus didn't stop doing and teaching things after he went back to heaven.

He still speaks and acts now, through his Spirit. His work on the cross is finished, but his kingdom ministry continues in and through the lives of believers. "For we are God's handiwork, created in Christ Jesus to do good works, which God prepared in advance for us to do" (Ephesians 2:10).

Sharing in His Story

In John 14:9–11, Jesus told his disciples that living as the Son means doing the will of the Father and that though they saw the Son working, what they really witnessed was the Father, indwelling the Son, doing his work through him.

To paraphrase, Jesus was saying, "I have no authority of my own. My Father is my authority. I speak what the Father tells me and I do what the Father shows me. I am in the Father and the Father is in me, so the Father does his work in and through me."

The same is true for sons and daughters of grace, Jesus continued (John 14:12–14, 20; 17:21). In essence, he's saying, "To live as a child of God is to do my Father's will. But know this: You are in me and I am in you, so I do my Father's work in and through you. If you're in union with me, you'll know what to ask of me, and I will do it—and so glorify my Father. I will live my life of sonship in and through you and you'll share in my work."

Believers participate in the present-day ministry of Jesus to the church and to the world. What a privilege!

Ministry (serving people to the glory of God) is something all believers do, not just pastors. The pastor's job is to equip believers for the work of ministry (Ephesians 4:11–12). God has called every one of us to this task.[34]

It's not really *our* ministry, though. It's Christ's. Our part is to continue the kingdom work of Jesus and it begins when we allow him to minister to us, in us and through us by his Spirit. His ministry, not ours, blesses and restores those to whom we minister.

Accepting this message requires a lot of humility, but it's liberating, because it removes the onus of having to strive to make things happen. It's not up to us. Christ bears the entire burden on his shoulders. Our calling is simply to share in his life. We can rest in him, the true and faithful minister (Matthew 11:28–30).

The Christian life is not about our plans, but about our part in God's plan and Christ's ongoing story in the world (Acts 20:24). It's not our journey with a place for Christ, but Christ's journey with a place for us. Our life is a pilgrimage in his (Galatians 2:20).

If we view the story as our story, the ministry as our ministry, or the priority as ministry rather than Jesus, we risk succumbing to pride, independence, or jealousy toward other ministries that seem more successful than ours. We may experience anxiety, unhappiness or depression, even disillusionment or burnout.

Christ shares his mission with us so that through us he might continue to bless all people of the world, bringing the fullness of his life into the lives of the empty and broken.

Getting Started

We must begin and continue in Christ's ministry as Jesus did: with faith strengthened through prayer and Scripture. We need to trust the Father.

Our faith is a share in Jesus's faith (Hebrews 12:2). It's a participation in his heartfelt trust in the Father's love and goodness and in his dependence on the Father for guidance and empowerment by the Holy Spirit.

To Jesus, faith was essential. The same should be true for us (Proverbs 3:5–6; 2 Corinthians 5:7).

We mature in our faith through a prayer-fueled life, meditating on Scripture, and fellowship with other believers.

Prayer

We should soak our lives in prayer (1 Thessalonians 5:16–18) because prayer builds our faith (Jude 1:20; Philippians 4:6–7).

Prayer is conversation and communion with our Abba Father, who loves us. This is when we consciously seek God and adore him, praise him, thank him, confess to him, call on him, petition him, submit to him, quiet our hearts and minds to listen to him and enjoy his presence. We can ask God for a share in Christ's life and resources, whatever we need at the time. Prayer is the key to the kingdom of God coming into our midst with power.

When we pray "through Jesus" (John 14:13; Ephesians 2:18; Hebrews 13:15), we gain access to the Father's ear, but praying through Jesus is about more than mere access. It is an outflow of our union with Christ. It's a participation in the Son's conversation and communion with his Abba Father (Mark 14:36; Galatians 4:4–6), which always centers on seeking and submitting to the Father's will (Luke 22:42; John 6:38; Hebrews 10:7).

Whether spoken or sung to music, prayer is one of our finest experiences of sharing in the Son's fellowship of love and intimacy, joy and freedom, creativity and glory with the Father in the Spirit. When we pray, we enter into the prayer life of Jesus in the power of the Holy Spirit.

Scripture

Faith is also strengthened through Scripture. Only through God's Word can we know the truth about God and his promises, his plan and his will. It is nourishment for our soul. In the written Word we encounter the living Word of God. As Jesus said, "Man shall not live on bread alone, but on every word that comes from the mouth of God" (Matthew 4:4).

The Christian who lives life without God's written Word is like a ship without a rudder. Having no direction, he drifts wherever the currents of the world take him.

Fellowship

Faith is strengthened through fellowship with other believers.

A deep sense of togetherness typified the first Christians. Daily they devoted themselves to the apostles' teaching and to mutual support, the Lord's Supper and prayer (Acts 2:42). They exercised spiritual gifts (1 Corinthians 14:26), carried each other's burdens (Galatians 6:2) and shared possessions with brothers and sisters in need (Acts 2:45). Their lives radiated the beauty of koinonia. Selflessly, they displayed love and loyalty, compassion and comfort, tenderness and humility (Philippians 2:1–5) so that the church was built up (Romans 15:1–2; 1 Corinthians 14:26).

When our hearts are knit together in Christ, we embrace and encourage one another in love and our faith is enriched.

Equipped

Furnished with Christ's faith—strengthened through prayer, Scripture, and fellowship—we're equipped to participate in Christ's ongoing ministry to the nations.

Set Your Mind on Things Above

If we want to become like Jesus in life and ministry, we must think like him.

The mind governs behavior and fashions character (Romans 8:5). Thoughts lead to desires, attitudes and feelings as well as to action. The devil knows this—which is why he preys on our thoughts, making the mind the main battlefield of life's great war (1 Peter 5:8–9).

We must guard our minds and our hearts since everything we do flows from there (Proverbs 4:23). We should set them on the things of Christ (Philippians 4:8; Colossians 3:1–3).

The Holy Spirit in us fights to keep our eyes on Jesus and his kingdom purpose (John 16:14–15). The Spirit helps us discipline our minds against the flesh (Romans 8:6; 2 Timothy 1:7). Specifically, the Spirit brings Christ to us, renewing our minds with his. The renewed mind (Romans 12:2; Ephesians 4:23) participates in the thought life of Jesus (1 Corinthians 2:16; Philippians 2:1–8).

We would do well, therefore, to ask the Father daily to sanctify our minds with the mind of Jesus. Ask him to purify your thoughts with Christ's thoughts and to make the desires of Christ's heart those of your heart too.

Ministering Love

When we share in the mindset of Christ through union with him, spiritual fruit (Galatians 5:22–23) and spiritual gifts (1 Corinthians 12:1–11) become evident in our lives (Philippians 2:1–8). The greatest of these is love (1 Corinthians 12:31–13:13; Colossians 3:14).

We're told in 1 John 4:8 that "God is love." At the heart of God is love. The Father loves the Son in the Spirit. The Son reciprocates with love for the Father in the Spirit. The Holy Spirit binds the Father and Son together in love. The triune God is always others-focused.

When the Son lived as a human on earth, fulfilling the will of his Father with a deep sensitivity to the Spirit, his life radiated love for God and humanity. He showed *agapē*—the supremely self-sacrificing love seen in God's love for the world (John 3:16).

God, who desires us to be conformed to the image of his Son, calls us to a selfless life of *agapē* love (John 13:34; 1 John 3:16). This is not warm feelings or tenderness toward someone (as in *philía* or brotherly love, to which we're also called), but a life of self-effacing, self-sacrificing actions for the sake of other people (Philippians 2:1–8). In every situation, in love we're to put others first and ourselves last.

Only one human being lived completely selflessly, so there's only one way for us to show *agapē* love: through union with Christ. The key is not imitation of Jesus, nor the keeping of a law, so much as sharing in his life of love.

If our lives don't express *agapē* love, the mind of Christ is not in us.

Agapē love is our highest calling (Matthew 22:37–40; John 13:34–35). It's the centerpiece of worship and ministry. "Do everything in love," Paul says (1 Corinthians 16:14). For where such love exists, people are made whole and God is glorified.

Sharing the Wounds of Christ

Jesus's entire human life involved suffering. In every instance, he matured through what he experienced. He embraced his afflictions all the way to the cross, to the glory of his Father, and through it all he himself was perfected (Hebrews 2:10; 5:7–9) and glorified (Luke 24:26–27).

Jesus is victor, not in spite of his travails, but through them. We see this most profoundly in his resurrection from the dead.

To have the mind of Christ is to embrace suffering (Matthew 5:10–12). This is a bitter pill to swallow. Most Christians would rather be united with the comforts of this world than with the sufferings of Christ.

Scripture tells us the apostles rejoiced in their tribulations (Romans 5:3; James 1:2; 1 Peter 4:13). How can anyone in their right mind embrace adversity and hardship, much less rejoice in it? The disciples believed they suffered for Jesus (Acts 5:41) and with Jesus (2 Corinthians 4:10). They grasped that the greater their suffering for Christ, the more intense was their communion with him. They understood that they were sharing in Christ's sufferings (Romans 8:17; 2 Corinthians 1:5; Philippians 3:10; 1 Peter 4:13).

The apostles did not rejoice in masochistic delight because of the trial itself, but because of what it produces: perseverance, character and hope (Romans 5:3–5). Ultimately, maturity in Christ (James 1:2–4). They knew the good and the glory that God could bring out of their anguish (1 Peter 4:12–16, 19).

As Christians, we will suffer (Matthew 5:10–11; 24:9; John 15:18–21; 16:33; Acts 14:22; Philippians 1:29; 2 Timothy 3:12; James 1:2; 1 Peter 4:12–19). Jesus told us, "A servant is not greater than his master" (John 15:20). If Jesus suffered, we will suffer also, in him. Embracing and rejoicing in this goes against human instinct.

But if we understand God's wisdom in human affliction, we'll find solace whenever we find ourselves in its midst. "For just as we share abundantly in the sufferings of Christ, so also our comfort abounds through Christ" (2 Corinthians 1:5).

Adversity and pain ought to draw us closer to God. When Jesus faced hostility or inner struggle, he offered himself to his Abba Father in the power of the Holy Spirit (Mark 14:32–36; Hebrews 9:14). Suffering is meant to intensify our communion with the triune God. Sharing in the sufferings of the Son, we're to trust in the Father and submit to him by the Spirit.

We are to share in Jesus's sufferings so that through identification with the trials and wounds of Christ we might know him more deeply and mature into his likeness. If we're like him in his trials, we'll be like him in his glory, and the Father will be glorified in and through it all. So in Christ, we can embrace the weakness and brokenness of our humanity and accept affliction even when we feel utterly, unbearably crushed by it.

Trials can arise from a variety of causes.

Many will be due to our faith in Christ—suffering for his name's sake. The message of the cross is a scandal to the world. It's a stumbling block to the Jews and foolishness to everyone else, until they come to believe (1 Corinthians 1:18–25). The world will persecute us for promoting the gospel. We'll be hated and rejected, as Jesus was. Every time Jesus has been lifted up by the church, satanic hostility has broken out. Christians have been attacked and spat upon, even martyred.

In our pursuit of holiness, we're tempted. We wrestle with sin and evil. The demonic powers that are opposed to the glory of God revealed in Jesus Christ will engage in intense spiritual warfare against us.

We suffer because we're united with Christ (Philippians 3:10–11). This does not necessarily mean physical pain, but typically involves the agony of letting go of things we treasure in submission to the Father's will.

Other afflictions involve the troubles and hardships common to all human beings living in a broken world wracked by anguish and conflict, weariness and sickness, hurt and grief (Romans 8:18–25).

Christians are called to be conformed to the image of God's Son (Romans 8:29). In our union with him we'll participate in his sufferings. Because in God's wisdom, suffering is the gateway to glory.

Jesus was perfected and glorified through trials. We grow in spiritual maturity the same way (Romans 5:3–4; Hebrews 12:5–11; James 1:2–4). Through the fires of suffering, the hand of God refines and purifies us.

What areas of your life are points of stress or struggle for you at present? These are most likely the growth areas where God is working in you for your sanctification. Through your brokenness, God matures you.

Anticipate suffering, but expect breakthrough, victory and transformation. Christ's resurrection power is always operative in us when we participate in his afflictions (Philippians 3:10–11).

"We share in Christ's sufferings," says Paul, "in order that we may also share in his glory" (Romans 8:17). "Our light and momentary troubles are achieving for us an eternal glory that far outweighs them all" (2 Corinthians 4:17).

And so, as John Stott puts it: "We rejoice not only in the end (glory), but in the means to the end (suffering). We rejoice in them both."[35]

The greatest reason for Christ's suffering, and ours, isn't about our glory but God's. He is glorified through our trials as we faithfully respond to them with the character of Jesus.

Unless we understand this divine wisdom, the way we view hardship will be no different from how nonbelievers view it. We'll be traumatized by misery and loss, becoming bitter and twisted, because we'll see no purpose in our difficult circumstances. We'll do all we can to resist life's thorns and brambles.

Of course, there's nothing wrong with praying for God to take away your suffering and that of others. Even Jesus in Gethsemane asked for the cup to be taken from him. But we should add, as Jesus did, "May the Father's will ultimately be done" (Matthew 26:39; Luke 22:42).

The Father never promised the absence of suffering, only the presence of Christ. God does some of his greatest work in us in our deepest, darkest times.

Conclusion

Unshakable Joy

In John 15:1–11, Jesus reveals an astounding truth about the joy of being united with him.

Jesus desires that "my joy may be in you and that your joy may be complete" (15:11). He isn't saying simply, "I want you to be full of joy." He's saying, "I want you to experience *my joy*—that irrepressible elation I experience deep within my soul."

The glorious gift Jesus shares with us is his relationship with the Father and their deep fellowship of mutual love. Intimacy with Abba is the source of his eternally abounding joy—which can be our experience as well.

In Christ we can have unshakable joy at all times (John 17:13), even in a broken world beset by fear, anxiety and suffering, where war ravages, sickness plagues and evil lurks around every corner. And even in a foolish world rife with secularism, pluralism, relativism, consumerism, individualism and countless other cultural diseases. In a greedy, cutthroat, dog-eat-dog world where stress, busyness and tiredness have become the accepted norm. We can, as Paul exhorts, "rejoice in the Lord always" (Philippians 4:4).

The more we focus on the person of Jesus and our oneness with him, the more thrilling the gospel becomes and the more meaningful life becomes. In Christ the floodgates of God's love and grace have been opened, never to close.

You'll fall deeper in love with your Abba Father as the Spirit takes you deeper into the life and heart of Jesus. His joy will be in you.

You will glimpse the wonder and mystery of the gospel and celebrate God's great embrace.

Questions for Reflection and Discussion

Introduction—Life Is All About Jesus

1. Think of one sentence from the Introduction that resonated with you. Why was it meaningful to you?
2. What inspires you most about the lives of the apostles?
3. What is your reaction to the idea that life is all about Jesus? Do you feel excited, surprised, disappointed, confused?
4. Jesus is within us and we're in him. What do you think this means?
5. Do you believe salvation is a free gift from God? If not, how would it affect your day-to-day life to know that you cannot save yourself and that you must rely solely on God's grace in Christ?

Chapter 1—A Grace Awakening

1. What insights did you discover in this chapter?
2. Martin Luther described the gospel as "the joyous exchange."[36] John Calvin called it "the wonderful exchange."[37] What is this exchange

and how does it benefit us? Does this truth encourage and excite you? Why?

3. Read Ephesians 1:3. What spiritual blessings have you been given in Christ?

4. Jesus shares everything of his with us. How does knowing this affect your relationship with God and your daily life? What would it look like for you to rest in this promise today?

5. God sees our whole life, from birth to death and beyond. But governed as we are by time, we can't see the end from the beginning. We need the Father's constant reassurance. Did you find the dialogue at the end of this chapter between a Christian and God to be comforting? If so, in what ways?

Chapter 2—The Gospel in Two Words

1. What are the key things you learned from this chapter?

2. What does it mean to be "in Christ"?

3. What was your initial reaction to the biblical truth of union with Christ? Have you come across this concept before?

4. Why should union with Christ be considered one of the most important teachings in the Bible? Why is it significant to know that you are in Christ and he is in you?

5. What practical steps could you take to encourage other believers to discover their union with Christ?

Chapter 3—The Dynamic of God

1. Do you believe that Jesus was able to perform miracles only because he's God? Why or why not?
2. According to Scripture, how do the three persons of the Trinity work in creation, in the life and death of Jesus, and in our lives today?
3. In what ways is it helpful for you to think of God's activity in terms of the Trinitarian dynamic described in this chapter (from the Father, through the Son, by the Spirit, for the Father)?
4. How would you describe the difference between *diversity* and *union*? Why is our relationship with God not a diversity?

Chapter 4—One with Jesus

1. In John 15:1–8, Jesus uses the picture of a vine and branches to help explain the revelation of our union with Christ. In Ephesians 5:31–32, Paul compares this truth to a marriage. Which metaphor speaks more clearly to your heart? Do you believe that you are one with Jesus? Why or why not?
2. How does your understanding of union with Christ deepen your relationship with God?
3. How did the first four chapters of this book change or challenge your view of how God relates to you?

Chapter 5—Our Father Wound

1. In what ways did this chapter resonate with you?

2. What feelings or thoughts come into your heart and mind when you think about your earthly father?

3. Do you have a father wound? If so, how has it been spiritually destructive in your life?

4. In what ways have you ever struggled with the idea that God is your Father?

5. In what ways might you have viewed God's fatherhood through the veil of your earthly father?

Chapter 6—Amelie and the Beloved

1. What moved you most in the story of baby Amelie? How can you find encouragement from her story?

2. How would you describe the greatness of the Father's love for his Son? How does knowing this help or comfort you?

3. How did this chapter affect your understanding of God's nature or character?

Chapter 7—Abba's Child

1. What part of this chapter affected you the most? Why?

2. How do you define yourself? In what ways have you looked to your work, family, achievements, possessions, or something else to satisfy the cry of your heart for a sense of identity and belonging? How does God define you?

3. What does it mean to you that you share in the sonship of Jesus? What can you do to

remind yourself of your true identity as Abba's precious child?

4. Think about this statement: *Nothing I've done or haven't done—and nothing I'm doing or not doing, or might or might not do—can ever make Abba love me any more or any less.* Do you agree or disagree? Why?

5. Is there anything about yourself that you're struggling to accept? What would your Abba Father say to you about this? Are there any lies your mind has accepted that feed your insecurities? Hand them to your Abba Father in prayer and be encouraged by your true self-worth in Christ.

Chapter 8—The Greatest Love Story

1. What part of this chapter did you find most profound? Why?

2. Does the idea that Christians share in the life of the Trinity encourage, puzzle, bother, or surprise you? Why?

3. How would your daily life be different if you were convinced that you are Abba's child, adopted into the life of the Trinity?

4. Which statement do you think is most true:
   a) Believers go out *from* God's presence into the world.
   b) Believers go out *in* God's presence into the world.
   Practically speaking, how would you describe the difference in those two?

5. In what ways have the last few chapters of this book changed your view of who you are, or deepened your relationship with God?

Chapter 9—Sisyphus in the Church

1. How do you view your relationship with God and your Christian life?
2. Have you ever felt as though God withdrew his love or favor toward you after you sinned? When you sin, do you believe God becomes angry with you or turns his face away from you? What does the Bible say about this and how can you align your thoughts and feelings with that?
3. Do you sometimes live as if the only way you can be made right with God is by living a holy life? How can you change your perspective about this to align with what the Bible says?
4. Is there a legalist hiding in you? Do you sometimes have difficulty accepting how gracious and loving God is? How can you help your heart see God in a more biblical way?

Chapter 10—Freedom

1. What is the most significant thing you gained from this chapter?
2. What did Jesus accomplish in his life and on the cross? How does this truth speak to you right now?
3. How does it affect you to know that Jesus went through agony of body, soul and spirit for you?

How does it affect you to realize that this act of love for you by the Son was pre-eminently the *Father's* act? How does reflecting on the cross affect your sense of being loved and accepted by God?

Chapter 11—Forgiven

1. What did you think of Horatio Spafford's story? How would you compare his relationship with God to your own?
2. What does God's forgiveness mean to you? How does it affect you at a personal level?
3. Do you believe that God doesn't count your sins against you (as 2 Corinthians 5:19 tells us), and that he has removed your sin from you as far as the east is from the west (Psalm 103:12)? Do you feel fully and completely forgiven? If not, what sin do you think hasn't been forgiven and why?
4. Do you agree that we can't out-sin the cross of Christ? Why or why not?
5. Are there any untruths you've been believing about God or your relationship with him? What can you do to impart truth to your heart and mind?

Chapter 12—Positively Righteous

1. What struck you most forcefully in this chapter? In what way did it impact you?
2. What does justification mean to you? Why is union with Christ so crucial to our justification?

3. How does it make you feel to know you're justified through faith, by grace, in Christ alone? How does knowing that you share in the righteousness of Jesus affect the way you relate to God and approach him in prayer?

4. Do you agree that "being comes before doing"? In what ways have you seen this in action? In what ways have you tried the reverse? What were the results from each instance?

5. Do you feel liberated by the truths mentioned in this chapter? How does knowing about them affect your relationship with God? How do they affect your daily Christian life?

Chapter 13—Fear Is Gone

1. Which truth mentioned in this chapter do you most need to take to heart right now?

2. When have you felt the conviction of the Holy Spirit? Have you ever felt as if God were condemning you? How can you tell the difference? Which do you think is the truth?

3. How have the past few chapters changed or challenged your view of what God thinks of you? Can you approach God with peace, confidence and freedom? Why or why not?

Chapter 14—The Call to Discipleship

1. Do you agree that grace is risky? In what ways is it possible for people to abuse God's grace?

2. How can you become more like Jesus in your character? Can you look back on your life and see evidence or fruit of God's sanctifying work?

3. How does knowing your position in Christ bring you freedom? How does it help you to live a selfless life like Jesus?

Chapter 15—Glorifying God

1. What is the meaning of life from your perspective?

2. Have you ever struggled to find your life's purpose? If so, describe your thoughts, longings, and struggles.

3. Do you worship God, enjoy him, delight in him? What does it mean to you to worship and glorify God?

4. How do you share in the Son's life of worship?

5. What areas of your life do you still need to surrender to God?

Chapter 16—Life's Great War

1. What did you learn about yourself from this chapter?

2. What tactics does Satan use in his spiritual battle against you and your relationship to God?

3. Think of an area of your life in which Satan attacks and often wins. In what ways could you better equip yourself to fight him to victory? How does knowing that Jesus has already defeated the enemy affect the way you approach this battle?

4. What struggle does Paul describe in Romans 7:15–24? Do you see a similar struggle in your own life? In verse 25, what is Paul's answer to the problem of self-reliance? How can you apply that to your situation?

5. Do you have an attitude of gratitude toward God? Has it been the main inspiration in your worship? Do you see any problem with that perspective?

Chapter 17—Living Christ's Life

1. What part of this chapter had the most impact on you? How would your life be different if you applied this insight to yourself?

2. Jesus has already lived our Christian life for us and now he reproduces his life in us. How does this truth speak to you right now?

3. Before reading this chapter, did you realize that you share by faith in all the life and resources of Jesus? If you truly believed that, what difference could it make in your thoughts, attitudes, and actions?

4. Select one of Christ's resources from his life of sonship that is relevant to a situation you're currently experiencing. Have you prayerfully sought to share in this resource? If not, stop and do so now.

5. Can you say, along with Paul, "I no longer live, but Christ lives in me" (Galatians 2:20)? How can believing that Jesus lives within you help you to worship and glorify the Father in your everyday activities and situations?

6. How do you feel about sharing in Christ's life of sonship by living the selfless, sacrificial life he did? What would that look like for you in practical terms? In what ways would it affect the way you relate to others?

Chapter 18—Life in the Spirit

1. The Bible declares that we're empowered for Christian living by the Holy Spirit, who indwells us. (Read John 14:26; Romans 8:26; Galatians 5:16, 18, 25; Ephesians 3:16; and 2 Timothy 1:14.) In what ways have you experienced the Holy Spirit's power in your Christian life? In what areas could you benefit from more of this power?

2. How did you see the Spirit's work, fruit and gifts expressed in your life this week? How do you think you can learn to live more "by the Spirit"?

3. In what ways does it help you to know that God doesn't demand perfection from you, but he desires your heart to passionately pursue him?

Chapter 19—United We Stand

1. What are some ways that individualism and consumerism undermine your church family, your Christian fellowship and your spiritual growth?

2. Do you know some Christians who feel bored or passionless about church? Have you yourself become disillusioned with church? Did your

attitude toward church change as you read this chapter about the church's union with Christ? How can you influence others who feel negatively about church?

3. Why do you think some Christians feel inferior to others in the body of Christ? How could an understanding of their union with Christ encourage these people?

4. What can you do to cultivate a fuller sense of *koinonia* in your local church and small group? Can you think of a brother or sister in Christ who has a pressing need for fellowship? In what practical ways can you come alongside to help or support this person?

5. What gift of the Spirit has the Father given you for sharing in Christ's ongoing kingdom ministry to the church and the world? Do you sometimes avoid exercising this gift from a fear of rejection? Since you have access to Christ's life and resources, how can knowing this embolden you in sharing your gifts with others?

Chapter 20—Kingdom Ministry

1. How do you picture God, yourself, and the act of prayer when you are speaking with God? When you pray, do you see yourself as Abba's child, sharing in the prayers of the Son to his Father?

2. Give this prayer a try throughout this week: "Father, please lay upon my heart the things

that are on yours." How could this change your perspective on prayer?

3. Think of some situations in which you could show Christ's *agapē* love to others this week. What would this involve? What might be the results?

4. Do you see ways in which your present suffering is bringing you to maturity in Christ? How can you find purpose and joy in the pain?

5. How have the past several chapters impacted your daily life and your relationship with God?

Conclusion—Unshakable Joy

1. How has this book moved you forward in your walk with God?

2. What does it mean to you to be one with Christ—to be in Christ and to have him within you? Does what you read in this book about your union with Christ change the way you view God and relate to him? Does it affect how you view yourself, how you go about life, and how you relate to others?

3. How could you encourage your friends with the insights you've learned from this book?

4. Declare these words over your life:

I am one with Jesus. I'm in him and he lives within me. At all times, I can rest in Christ, rely on him, and draw on his resources through my union with him. In him I share in all that he is and has. All manner of blessings and promises are mine to enjoy. All the burning needs and questions of my existence find perfect satisfaction. I have everything I could ever need—in him. I can have joy and contentment in all things because I have Jesus.

Praise God!

Notes and References

1   I've long since lost the article describing Luther's understanding of salvation as a "wonderful" or "joyous exchange." However, there are plenty of books that note this concept in Luther's theology. For example, Robert Kolb and Charles P. Arand, *The Genius of Luther's Theology: A Wittenberg Way of Thinking for the Contemporary Church* (Grand Rapids: Baker Academic, 2008), 46.

2   See Martin Luther, "The Freedom of a Christian, 1520," in *Luther's Works: Career of the Reformer: I*, edited by Harold J. Grimm, general editor Helmut T. Lehmann; translated by W.A. Lambert, revised by Harold J. Grimm (Philadelphia: Fortress Press, 1957), volume 31, pages 351–352; Martin Luther, "Two Kinds of Righteousness, 1519" in *Luther's Works: Career of the Reformer: I*, edited by Harold J. Grimm, general editor Helmut T. Lehmann; translated by Lowell J. Satre (Philadelphia: Fortress Press, 1957), volume 31, page 297.

3   See Bruce Demarest, *The Cross and Salvation: The Doctrine of Salvation* (Wheaton, Illinois: Crossway, 1997), 313.

4   Albert Schweitzer, *The Mysticism of Paul the Apostle* (Baltimore: John Hopkins University Press, 1998), 3.

5   James S. Stewart, *A Man in Christ: The Vital Elements of St. Paul's Religion* (Vancouver, British Columbia: Regent College, 2002), 147.

6   Brennan Manning, *Abba's Child: The Cry of the Heart for Intimate Belonging* (Colorado Springs: NavPress, 2015), 108.

7   See Martyn Lloyd-Jones, *God the Holy Spirit* (Wheaton, Illinois: Crossway, 1997), 102–103.

8 Sinclair B. Ferguson, *The Christian Life: A Doctrinal Introduction* (Edinburgh, Scotland: The Banner of Truth Trust, 1981), 97.

9 See John Murray, *Redemption: Accomplished and Applied* (Grand Rapids: Eerdmans, 1955), 161.

10 See Sinclair B. Ferguson, *The Holy Spirit* (Downers Grove, Illinois: InterVarsity, 1996), 108.

11 Daniel Montgomery and Timothy Paul Jones, *PROOF: Finding Freedom through the Intoxicating Joy of Irresistible Grace* (Grand Rapids: Zondervan, 2014), 97.

12 Sinclair B. Ferguson, *By Grace Alone: How the Grace of God Amazes Me* (Sanford, Florida: Reformation Trust, 2010), 102.

13 See W.A. Criswell, *Expository Sermons on Revelation: Volume Two* (Grand Rapids: Zondervan, 1963), 183–184.

14 Brennan Manning, *Abba's Child: The Cry of the Heart for Intimate Belonging* (Colorado Springs: NavPress, 2015), 148.

15 See J. I. Packer, *Knowing God* (London: Hodder & Stoughton, 1973), 182.

16 Bernard of Clairvaux, "Sermon 8, The Holy Spirit: The Kiss of the Mouth," in *The Works of Bernard of Clairvaux, Volume Two: Song of Songs I*, Cistercian Fathers Series: Number Four, edited by M. Basil Pennington; translated by Kilian Walsh (Trappist, Kentucky: A Cistercian Publications title published by Liturgical Press, 1971), 46.

17 See Robert Graves, *Greek Myths* (London: Penguin, 1981), 63–64.

18 See Robert Harvey, *Best-Loved Hymn Stories* (Grand Rapids: Zondervan, 1963), 158–160; Kenneth W. Osbeck, *101 Hymn Stories* (Grand Rapids: Kregel, 1982), 126–128.

19 Martin Luther, "Scholia: Chapter Four" in *Luther's Works: Lectures on Romans*, edited by Hilton C. Oswald; translated by Jacob A. O. Preus (Saint Louis, Missouri: Concordia Publishing House, 1972), volume 25, page 260.

20 See John R. W. Stott, *Men Made New: An Exposition of Romans 5–8* (Leicester, U.K.: InterVarsity, 1966), 36.

21 It's worth noting a popular misunderstanding of Paul's key phrase of Romans 6, "died to sin." Unfortunately, some see "died to sin" in the context of sanctification rather than justification. As John Stott explains, the misinterpretation goes something like this: A person who has "died to sin" is unresponsive to it. That is, they're as unresponsive to the

temptation of sin as a corpse is to physical stimulus. But as Stott himself points out in detail, there are good reasons why this interpretation cannot be correct. For example, our own personal experience ought to be proof enough that our sinful nature is still alive and kicking. What's more, if we're unresponsive or insensitive to sin, if we have no desire or inclination to sin because we've died to it, then Paul's concluding exhortations that we not sin are completely unnecessary (Romans 6:12–14)—and so is every other passage of Scripture exhorting us not to sin. Contextually, the "unresponsive to sin" explanation makes no sense. See John R. W. Stott, *Men Made New: An Exposition of Romans 5–8* (Leicester, U.K.: InterVarsity, 1966), 37–41; John R. W. Stott, *The Message of Romans* (Leicester, U.K.: InterVarsity, 1994), 169–171.

22 See John R. W. Stott, *Men Made New: An Exposition of Romans 5–8* (Leicester, U.K.: InterVarsity, 1966), 30–52; John R. W. Stott, *The Message of Romans* (Leicester, U.K.: InterVarsity, 1994), 168–182.

23 See Martin Luther, "To Jerome Weller. July, 1530," in *Luther: Letters of Spiritual Counsel*, Library of Christian Classics edition, translated and edited by Theodore G. Tappert (Vancouver, British Columbia: Regent College, 1960), 86–87.

24 For insightful explanations of Romans 6:1–14 see John R. W. Stott, *Men Made New: An Exposition of Romans 5–8* (Leicester, U.K.: InterVarsity, 1966), 30–52 (the biography illustration I describe is from pages 49–50); John R. W. Stott, *The Message of Romans* (Leicester, U.K.: InterVarsity Press, 1994), 168–182; Sinclair B. Ferguson, *By Grace Alone: How the Grace of God Amazes Me* (Sanford, Florida: Reformation Trust, 2010), chapter 7.

25 See John R. W. Stott, *Men Made New: An Exposition of Romans 5–8* (Leicester, U.K.: InterVarsity, 1966), 50, 56.

26 See John Calvin, *Institutes of the Christian Religion*, Library of Christian Classics edition, edited by John T. McNeill, translated by Ford Lewis Battles (Louisville: Westminster John Knox, 1960), III.xvi.1; John Calvin, *Calvin's Commentaries: The First Epistle of Paul the Apostle to the Corinthians*, edited by David W. Torrance and Thomas F. Torrance, translated by John W. Fraser (Grand Rapids: Eerdmans, 1960), 46.

27 Mark Twain, *Mark Twain Speaking*, edited by Paul Fatout (Iowa City: University of Iowa Press, 1976), 284.

28 See John Piper, *Future Grace: The Purifying Power of the Promises of God* (Colorado Springs: Multnomah, 2012), 3.

29 Quotations from J. Hudson Taylor in this chapter are from "The Exchanged Life," a letter from Taylor in Chinkiang, China, dated 17 October 1869, to his sister Amelia Broomhall in England. This letter is reproduced in Taylor's biography, written by his son Howard and daughter-in-law Geraldine. See Dr. and Mrs. Howard Taylor, *Hudson Taylor and the China Inland Mission: The Growth of a Work of God* (London: China Inland Mission, 1927), 173–177.

30 Lewis B. Smedes, *Union with Christ: A Biblical View of the New Life in Jesus Christ* (Grand Rapids: Eerdmans, 1983), 58.

31 John R. W. Stott, *Life in Christ: A Guide for Daily Living* (London: Monarch, 2003), 125.

32 John R. W. Stott, *Basic Christianity* (Grand Rapids: Eerdmans, 2008), 123.

33 C. S. Lewis, *The Weight of Glory and Other Addresses* (New York: Simon & Schuster, 1980), 123.

34 See John Piper, *Future Grace: The Purifying Power of the Promises of God* (Colorado Springs: Multnomah, 2012), 287.

35 John R. W. Stott, *Men Made New: An Exposition of Romans 5–8* (Leicester, U.K.: InterVarsity, 1966), 15.

36 See Robert Kolb and Charles P. Arand, *The Genius of Luther's Theology: A Wittenberg Way of Thinking for the Contemporary Church* (Grand Rapids: Baker Academic, 2008), 46.

37 John Calvin, *Institutes of the Christian Religion*, Library of Christian Classics edition, edited by John T. McNeill, translated by Ford Lewis Battles (Louisville: Westminster John Knox, 1960), IV.xvii.2.

Index of Subjects and Names

Scripture Index

CPSIA information can be obtained
at www.ICGtesting.com
Printed in the USA
BVHW072353070522
636318BV00004B/13